KAJIRRI

Kajirri
The Bush Missus

Alexa Simmons

Edited by Darrell Lewis

First published in 2005 by Central Queensland University Press

Second published in 2012 by Boolarong Press, Salisbury, Brisbane, Australia.

National Library of Australia Cataloguing-in-Publication entry

Author:	Simmons, Lexie.
Title:	Kajirri : the bush missus / Alexa Simmons.
ISBN:	9781921920790 (pbk.)
Subjects:	Simmons, Lexie.
	Women--Northern Territory--Biography.
	Women--Northern Territory--Social conditions.
	Ranch life--Northern Territory--Victoria River Region.
	Victoria River Downs (N.T.)--History.
Dewey Number:	920.720994

Printed and bound by Watson Ferguson & Company, Salisbury, Brisbane, Australia.

In the interest of historical accuracy, I have used some expressions and terminology, which were common usage in the 1940s and 1950s, but may now be considered offensive to some people. For this reason I ask for the readers' indulgence and to accept that no hurt or offence is intended. I hope that all will enjoy reading this book as much as I have enjoyed writing it.

Lexie Simmons

Contents

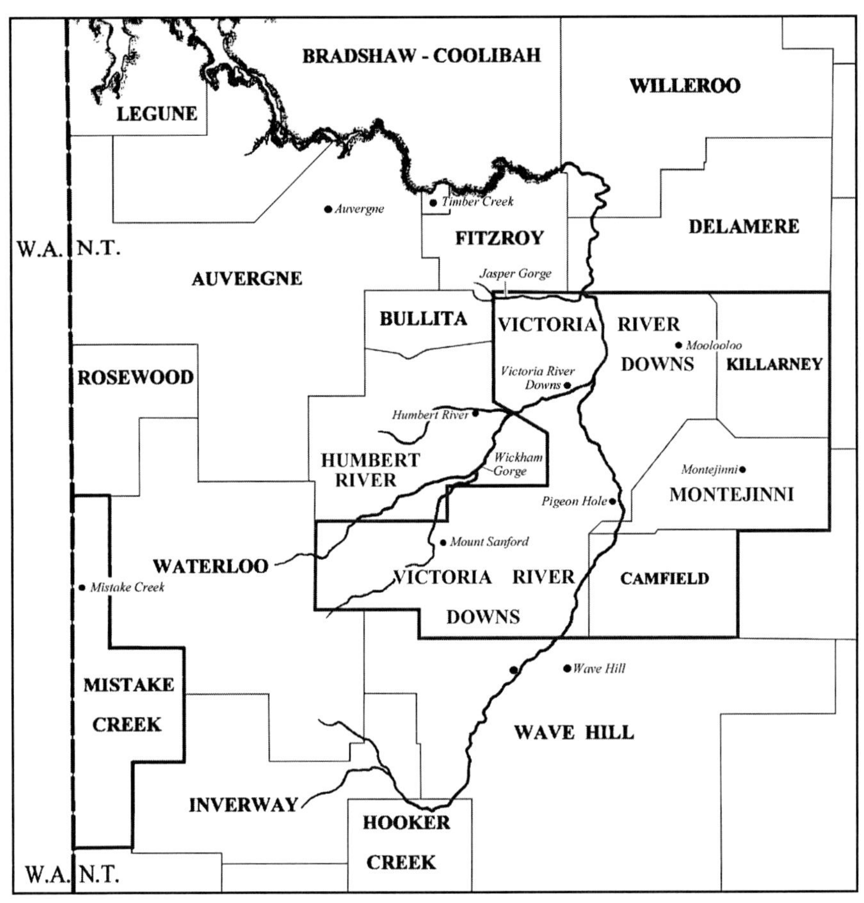

Regional map showing the location of Victoria River Downs and neighbouring cattle stations

Foreword

Mention the outback and most people would think of remoteness, wide open spaces, heat waves and droughts. And men! - stockmen, drovers, shearers, policeman, black trackers, miners, crocodile shooters and others. Every one knows the outback is a 'man's country'. But there were women in the outback, too - black women and white. White women have lived in the outback for generations, yet in the popular imagination and in the bulk of outback literature, they are overshadowed by men. Fortunately, with books like *Kajirri, the Bush Missus*, this situation is changing.

Lexie Simmons grew up in the genteel suburbs of Adelaide. The youngest in a family of seven, she led a very sheltered and protected life and always had important decisions made for her. In 1948 at the age of 23, another decision was made for Lexie, a decision which was to set the course of her life. Her family told her she was to travel from Adelaide to join her sister on the huge and famous Northern Territory cattle station, Victoria River Downs (VRD).

At this time VRD operated on the open range system. There was virtually no fencing and the cattle were wild and uncontrolled. Up to 20,000 wild bulls roamed the station and the stockmen wore guns to shoot the bulls - and to maintain their authority over the Aborigines.

Lexie's visit was meant to be short, a year or two at most, but fate intervened. A year after she arrived she became the wife of VRD head stockman George Bates and the 'missus' at the remote Mt. Sanford outstation, and within five years the mother of four children. In common with many places in the North at this time, conditions at Mt. Sanford were amazingly primitive. There was no refrigeration, electricity, hot water, airstrip or radio communication. Cooking was done on a wood stove, and lighting was with kerosene and carbide lamps. There was also the culture shock of a naive young Adelaide girl coming into close contact with Aboriginal people for the first time.

Gradually Lexie adjusted to her new life. She learned to kill, butcher and salt down her own beef, to make soap, and to cook and make bread for twenty or more. She also had to 'doctor' the sick and injured, including her own children and herself. Lexie learnt to get along with the Aborigines, to be a 'missus' and to look after their welfare, but she eventually came to realise that they looked after her as much as she did them! Whenever possible she participated in station activities beyond the confines of the homestead - mustering, broncoing, repairing bores. She also learnt to deal with an increasingly unsatisfactory marriage.

The outback was a man's country, but it was a woman's country, too. Lexie's story, *Kajirri, the Bush Missus,* covers the broad sweep of life on an outback station from a woman's point of view. It adds a vital piece to the story of Victoria River Downs and more generally to the story of white women in the outback. It will be welcomed by all - men and women - who love Australia's remote inland country and its history.

Darrell Lewis
Canberra

PART 1

VICTORIA RIVER DOWNS

Into the Outback

You might think it was easy being a 'missus' on a remote outstation of Victoria River Downs in the 1950s, the only white woman for sixty miles. Well, you'd be wrong! In those days the tracks out to 'civilisation' were slow and rough, and for half the year impassable. Living conditions were primitive, and it was doubly hard when all the men were out in the stock camp. One time when they were away I had to shoot a killer so that the Aboriginal camp and I could have meat – yes, I had to do this sort of thing! – but when I went to get my rifle I found that my husband George had taken it out to the stock camp and left me the station ·303. Usually cattle killed for meat were shot from a tree, but I was then heavily pregnant with my second baby and didn't relish using such a high-powered gun from a tree. It was very heavy for me to hold and from previous experience I knew it kicked like a mule. I didn't know how I'd go firing it one-handed as I could do easily with my small gun. Nevertheless, I hauled myself into the tree and the girls handed up the ·303. The cattle were driven beneath me so I took a firm grasp of my tree, aimed the gun and pulled the trigger. Suddenly I was hanging by my arm from a small branch, looking down at a seething mass of terrified cattle, with the killer in its death throes in their midst! I hastily dropped the rifle and managed to scramble back into the tree, and stood there shaking like a leaf.

That damn gun had nearly blown me out of the tree! How I hung on I'll never know, and what I would've done if I'd fallen and been injured I don't know either. I was the only one who could work the pedal wireless and we were fifty or sixty miles across country from Wave Hill station, and there was no able-bodied man to make the trip. After this I refused to kill out of a tree when I was pregnant, and made them yard the cattle so I could sit safely on the rails to shoot one. My husband George wasn't very pleased about this. He said the smell of blood made it difficult to yard the wild cattle, but as far as I was concerned that was his problem. So how did I get to be a 'missus' on the great Victoria River Downs in the Northern Territory? Well, let me start at the beginning.

I was born and grew up in Adelaide, the youngest of seven. Helen was the oldest, sixteen years older than me, then came Malcolm, Margaret, Eustace, Gwenda,

Natalie and me. Being the youngest, the rest of the family always treated me as if I was a young child. They were still doing this even when I reached my twenties. To them I was 'Bubbie', and all my life I was told where to go, what to do and how to do it. I was also very shy and certainly rarely stuck up for myself. It didn't do me any good if I did – I was just overruled.

At the beginning of 1948 my sister Natalie took the position of governess on Victoria River Downs, a huge pastoral property in the Northern Territory and known far and wide as 'VRD'. She'd previously had a highly paid job with Charles Moores, a large department store in Adelaide, but because they refused to release her to join the Women's Air Force during the Second World War, Nat became determined to leave them. Now she'd written to mum asking if I could join her because she was very lonely. At VRD she was living in a cottage on her own, instead of with her employers as was usual.

I'd been delighted when Natalie had left home and gone to VRD. For years she'd made my life a misery by ridiculing anything I said, or by making smart remarks that made everyone laugh at me. Years later I realised this was a classic case of sibling jealousy – until I was born she'd been the centre of attention, and I'd come along and taken her place. As a result of Nat's attentions I became quite introverted and lacked confidence. Since she'd left I'd begun to come out of my shell. I had a good job and even had a boyfriend. The last thing I wanted to do was leave home and come under Nat's domination again, but I'd been offered the position of storekeeper at VRD and my family had decided I'd take the job to keep her company.

So, on the morning of August 28th 1948 (a Saturday) I was taken to Adelaide Airport and sent off to northern Australia. I won't go into great detail about my trip north. I'd never flown before so I was very nervous, but I certainly found the scenery below quite fascinating. We stopped at Alice Springs on a scorcher of a day and were provided with a meal of hot roast pork and all the trimmings. Then we flew on to Tennant Creek which was even hotter. After leaving Tennant my greasy pork lunch decided to leave me and from there on I had my head in a bag every stop. I've often wondered why anyone would serve such an unsuitable meal to poor unsuspecting passengers on such a hot day, especially in the days before air-conditioning and pressurised cabins in aircraft. We landed at Daly Waters, Katherine, and finally reached Darwin.

We touched down just after 7.30 pm, a flight of thirteen hours, and as I stepped from the plane onto the tarmac I seemed to walk into a great wall of heat. The tarmac had been cooking all day in the hot sun and was now radiating the heat back. It was ninety-nine degrees Fahrenheit and the humidity was one hundred percent as there'd been a small shower of rain just before we landed – pretty tough for a city girl fresh up from an Adelaide winter. I felt as though I had one of my grandma's flat irons on my head, and there just didn't seem to be enough oxygen in the air to breathe, so I hurried as quickly as I could towards the airport lounge. I thought it surely must be a few degrees cooler inside.

As I stepped through the doors a young policeman grabbed my arm and gave me a big fright. He said, 'You must be Nat's sister. She asked me to look after you. I'm Bill Hatch.' My heart dropped back into place and I breathed a big sigh of relief. Bill took me to pick up my luggage and then we went on a quick tour around Darwin, including down to beautiful Mindil beach. My flight from Darwin to Victoria River Downs didn't leave until Monday and I was put up for the weekend with a policeman and his wife whose names I can't remember.

All the houses at the police barracks were built on stilts and made completely of wood, with corrugated iron roofs. There were no verandas but all the walls were louvres that could be opened to allow an air flow. I found it strange to sleep under a mosquito net which restricted what little air flow there was and made the atmosphere even more stifling, but I didn't realise just how much worse it would be to have no net and to suffer the mosquitoes. I just couldn't get used to the humidity, and my clothes always seemed to be damp and clinging to my body. Even to have a shower didn't give much relief as the water was always warm, even at night. I couldn't make up my mind just which was worse, the cold wet weather of Adelaide and my chilblains, or the heat and humidity of Darwin with its discomfort of damp, clinging clothes. I just hoped it would be better out at VRD. I was soon to find out.

On Monday morning I caught the MacRobertson Miller plane to VRD. This was a twin-engine Avro Anson, and we bumbled along at a much slower rate than we had on Saturday's DC3. The early morning was beautifully cool, with lots of white fluffy clouds floating in the clear blue sky, but I wasn't in the mood to appreciate it. I was too anxious – what would I find at my new home? Would it be anything like the sheep stations I'd visited in the far north of South Australia?

First Days at VRD

When we arrived at VRD airstrip Natalie was waiting there to greet me, along with the station manager, Hartley Magnussen. It was quite a relief to see a familiar face once again and to not be on my own any more. We were soon on our way to the homestead across an area of bright red soil, though this changed to white as we passed through a stand of blue box gums. These trees are about ten to twelve feet tall with white, twisting, spreading branches and leaves of a hazy blue, and were the main source of wood for the kitchen fires on the station. We crossed the Wickham River, a beautiful stream with majestic trees lining its banks – paperbarks, wild figs, river gums and pandanus – and bushes growing thickly at the edge of the water beneath the trees. I later saw that the leaves of these shrubs turned red at the beginning of the wet season, and looked really beautiful in the sunlight. On the other side we turned downstream and went on to the homestead.

As we drove I couldn't help contrasting the stations I had known in South Australia with the country here. Down south the land was almost bare of grass, with mostly saltbush and bluebush for the stock to feed on, and indeed they grew very well on it. What I saw here was completely different. There were trees on the river banks which grew to a good size, and there were many species of smaller trees bordering the plains. Although the grass was now dry there was evidence that it grew prolifically in the wet season.

Victoria River Downs station was a big sprawling affair. The main building was, of course, the 'Big House'. This stood on its own in a large garden with plenty of large shade trees. It was built up off the ground on piles and there were about six steps up to the wide front veranda. As best I can remember there were three bedrooms, a dining room and lounge, and a kitchen. The only parts I was ever to see were the front veranda and lounge. Along side it stood the old homestead which was now the overseer's quarters. This had been built years before with timber milled on the station by a contractor named Sammy Green, and the small portable sawmill Sammy used had been bought by the station and still stood in one of the sheds. Another large shed close by the mill was the old blacksmith's shop and held a forge, though I never saw it used while I was there.

There was also a big store where I was to work, with a saddlery shop on one side and an office on the other, but the office had its own veranda which set it a little apart. Standing in front of my store in the grounds of the Big House was a small shed with a cement floor. I was told that the previous manager, Alf Martin was the previous manager and the first person to have a motorcar on the station, and he'd used this shed as a garage, but it was now a paint store. Two of Alf's sons had a contract to cart supplies from the railhead at Alice Springs to VRD and another son was the boss of the stockyards at the Wyndham Meatworks. At this time Alf was retired and living in Katherine, and he later died in Perth.

To the left of the main store was a row of sheds and garages, and on the end of this was a large empty building which later was used as a school, and for picture shows during the wet season. Behind them were the men's quarters. Next to the empty building was a row of cottages, with a fence running from the last house across a small open space to join up to the front fence of the main house. In the centre of this fence was the main entrance gate. Another fence ran from the side of Nat's cottage, across an open space to join up with the high netting which surrounded the tennis court in the main house grounds. There was a small gate set into it which faced the office. This enclosed space effectively excluded the Big House from the married quarters. The entrance to the Big House was through a white painted gate with a path leading beneath large poinciana trees to the front veranda. Another small gate was set into the garden fence alongside the tennis court, with a paved path running beside the courts to the overseer's quarters. Just outside the main front fence a large sheet of white canvas had been erected as a screen for the occasional pictures.

We arrived at the station in time for morning tea at the Big House and there I met Hartley's wife, Gwen, and their two small children, Robin and Pam. Nat was governess to these children and taught them lessons which came monthly from the correspondence school in Adelaide, a wonderful help in teaching the children of the outback. Now, of course, lessons are received from School of the Air, broadcast from the nearest large town, but even today this might be hundreds of miles away, and for some children it's the only contact they have for months on end with other children of their own age.

At the time of my arrival VRD was over twelve thousand square miles, and believed to be the largest cattle station in the world. It had vast areas of rich black-soil plains which grew Mitchell and Flinders grass, both excellent stock feed. The property was taken up in 1883, but in 1909 it was purchased by a British company, 'Bovril Australian Estates'. Bovril introduced its own brand on VRD, the famous 'bulls head' (♉), and it was company policy not to sell any livestock with this brand except the cattle they sent to the Wyndham meatworks, or those they sent on the hoof to Dajarra in Queensland. At Wyndham the company exported frozen carcases to Britain, and near Dajarra they owned a holding property called Morestone where the bullocks were rested after their long journey, and fattened for the southern market.

To operate efficiently VRD was divided into five outstations with a white head-stockman and a team of Aborigines at each one and an overseer at the main homestead who was in charge overall. One outstation was Gordon Creek, about twelve miles up river. Another was Mt. Sanford, a good sixty miles to the south-west over a very rough road and with the nearest neighbour being the police at Wave Hill. The most isolated was Pigeon Hole, on the banks of the Victoria River about twenty miles upstream from the main homestead. Montejinni was farther away from the head station, about eighty miles, but it was near the junction of four dirt roads – one from Newcastle Waters, one from Wave Hill, one from VRD homestead, and another from Delamere and Katherine. The road to VRD carried on through to the Timber Creek police station and all points west. Midway between Montejinni and the head station was the last outstation, Moolooloo. For weeks at a time no communication would occur between most of the outstations and VRD homestead. Today you can travel from London to VRD in less time than it took to ride from the head station to most of the out-stations.

VRD was so large that it was known affectionately as the 'Big Run', and its size gave rise to an amusing story. A man named Peter Milne was a pastoral consultant for the whole area from Wyndham to Arnhem Land, and he spent most of his time travelling around the stations. One day Peter was in Wyndham and there he met an American tourist who wanted to go to Katherine. The tourist said he wanted to see something of the country so he didn't want to fly, and he was delighted to accept the offer of a lift, on the understanding that various calls had to be made at properties along the way. They duly set out, and it took them two days to get to Timber Creek where they spent the night at the police station. All along the way the American kept asking what station they were travelling through as there were no fences, or signs on any boundaries.

The third day they set out and again and in the morning the usual question was asked. He received the reply, 'Victoria River Downs'. That afternoon he asked the question again and received the same answer. They spent that night at VRD homestead and in the morning after Peter's business there was settled they set off again. Along the road the American asked the same old question, and got the same old answer: 'VRD'. They pulled into Moolooloo outstation and camped the night and the next day they set off once more, and after travelling some distance the American was told again that they were *still* on VRD. By this time he was convinced the Aussie was pulling his leg, so he bet Peter fifty pounds they hadn't been travelling for two days on the same property. Peter accepted. Early that evening they pulled into Katherine and Peter drove straight to his office and invited the American to view the large pastoral map on the wall behind his desk. The poor fellow was astounded. 'Mah God', he said. 'Ah thought we had big spreads in Texas where ah come from, but that beats anything ah have ever seen!' He paid the fifty pounds quite happily and boasted he'd soon make up his loss when he got back home, and he asked for a copy of the pastoral map so he could prove his story.

Bovril still owned VRD in 1948 and soon after I arrived one of the directors came to visit the station. He was very pleased with himself because in Darwin he'd done a deal to buy all the empty forty-four gallon drums scattered along the Stuart Highway. These drums had contained the bitumen used to make the highway, but because of the residue of tar in the drums everyone considered them useless. This fellow envisioned them being filled with fat from the meatworks in Darwin which was expected to reopen in the near future. Apparently Bovril was negotiating to be partners in this venture, but unfortunately (or perhaps fortunately) for the director the meatworks never opened. I often wondered what Bovril did about all those empty drums.

The European stockmen on VRD spent most of their time in stock camps, mustering cattle by day and at night sleeping in their swags out under the stars. Most of them went long periods without seeing another white man, and had only Aborigines for company. Very rarely another white stockman was employed on the same out-station, or there was a white cook who also acted as a hut-keeper, and the isolation and the rough and arduous nature of their work led to a particular type of man, with a particular temperament. Their dominant characteristic was rugged individualism, and they were never very talkative except among their own kind. Many of them cohabited with Aboriginal women even though it was then against the law, and it was from these liaisons that many part-coloured children appeared. Their idea of a good life was to work on a station for nine months of the year and save all their money, and then go to the nearest town – Katherine or Wyndham – for a few weeks' spree. They'd give their station cheque to either the publican or the local store, and when the money ran out they'd be 'poured' onto a plane home.

On the whole these men were the salt of the earth, always very polite to any white women they came into contact with, and I was surprised to find out just how well educated some of them were. Some were even university graduates. When I arrived on VRD it was only three years after the end of the Second World War, and many men were still unable to find suitable employment in their chosen fields. They became station hands of one kind or another, and no matter what the privations or hardships, they had a job to do and did it well. Nowadays conditions have changed dramatically. Individualism still persists, but isolation is largely a thing of the past and you can't be called a pioneer now simply because you live a hundred miles from a town. Four-wheel-drive vehicles, light planes and helicopters, and greatly improved roads have shrunk the old distances. Now all the stations have normal telephones, satellite television, internet links, and most have their own light planes. And when it comes to mustering, most is now done by helicopters.

Hartley Magnussen was a man very full of his own importance and he was heartily disliked by most of the men. He was very 'standoffish' towards me, until I delivered a message from a family friend he'd once worked for as a bookkeeper on their sheep station in the far north of South Australia. From then on I was treated as worthy of his notice. In contrast, Mrs Magnussen was a delightful lady, a tiny little thing barely five feet high. I called her 'Muzz' as she was like a second mother to me, but Hartley was always the 'Lord of the Manor'. Needless to say, Nat and I much preferred the company of Frank Spencer, the overseer, and Roley Bowry, the saddler, and we had most of our meals with them in the main dining room at the overseers' quarters.

After morning tea Natalie took me to our cottage, and I was shocked! Everything was so primitive! I was not expecting anything fancy, but this was like something from 1900. It was a one-room corrugated iron building with wide verandas on all sides. The outer veranda walls were closed in with a wooden latticework, and there were canvas blinds to let down when it rained. In the room there was a large cupboard where Nat hung her clothes, and shelves which held our towels, sheets, hats and shoes. The other side of the room was fitted with a canvas cupboard which Nat and Roley Bowry had made for me. Nat told me to make sure all my things were kept inside as the crickets would eat them if given half a chance. On the wall between our cupboards stood a dressing table and another small table, which completed the furniture, except for two coconut fibre mats and one cloth one. Later I bought some cotton material from the store to make curtains for the cupboard, which brightened up the place considerably.

Outside there was a little wooden gate with a crazy stone path running up to the front veranda, and there was couch grass growing all around. There were four frangipani trees along the front fence and I was told two were pink and two were white, but they were too small to be in flower. Later I planted some poinsettia shrubs along the side fence between our cottage and our neighbours, Jack and Belle Roden. Jack was the station bookkeeper, but he and his wife were both in their seventies so they kept pretty much to themselves.

Attached to the back of the cottage was a small kitchen and a bathroom, and in between was a covered walkway. The bathroom was quite primitive. It had a cement floor that sloped towards the back so the water would run out onto the lawn, and there was a towel rack and a shelf to hold our toilet things. The only other items in the room were a tap and a shower, an ancient metal affair with a rose the size of a plate. Only cold water was available and this was fine during the hot weather, but during the cold dry season it was freezing! The kitchen had a small wood-burning stove, a wooden table and one wooden chair. There were shelves along one wall and an open cupboard made from kerosene cases to hold our plates and things. The only cups were large enamel pannikins that I soon grew used to because I was always thirsty in the heat. We had all our meals at the overseer's quarters and in our cottage we were quite content to have just a little tea, coffee and cocoa, sugar and powdered milk. We also kept some plain flour, cream of tartar and baking soda in case we wanted to make some scones or cake for ourselves.

At the cottage I met Long Nellie, our 'house girl'. I soon learnt that all the Aboriginal women who worked for the whites were called 'girls' or 'house girls', and the Aboriginal men were called 'boys'. If they had a specific job, this often was applied before 'boy' or 'girl'. For instance, the man who collected wood was called a 'wood boy', and one who always accompanied the manager as he drove around was called a 'car boy'. It was Nellie's duty to do the housework and to wash and iron our clothes, and she'd been well trained and took very good care of us. She was tall for an Aboriginal, about five foot ten and very slim, and she towered over both Nat and me. Her skin was quite dark, with a slight golden sheen, and she had very short jet-black hair that had a lovely blue-black tinge after it was washed. When she became excited she couldn't keep still and would dance from foot to foot, twisting her hands round and round each other.

Nellie was very shy at our first meeting, standing with one foot twisted behind the other and averting her gaze, but sneaking occasional glances as if assessing me. For myself, I felt uncomfortable with Nellie for several weeks because she was the first Aboriginal I'd met face to face. I didn't know what to say to her, so I left it to Nat to give her and other Aborigines any orders. All of them seemed to stand back assessing me, just as I was assessing them, and some even cringed when I came upon them unawares. For a while I couldn't understand this and it made me very uncomfortable, but as I settled in to my new surroundings I noticed the way some of the whites treated them, and I began to understand. I remembered one of the lessons my mother gave me as a child: 'A lady always treats everyone the same, and it's only her friends she treats as her intimates'. I also remembered how she used to treat our maid, Olga Clements, and I thought, 'I'll just treat the Aborigines like mum did Olga – firm, but kind'.

The floors of the cottage were made of cement and during the hot weather it was Nellie's job to hose the verandas down so it would be a little cooler for us in the evenings, and all the red dust that had blown in during the day was cleaned out. I don't think Nellie bothered to sweep the house each morning, but just washed all the dust away every afternoon. We were only in it to rest for an hour after lunch so it didn't matter much. Our lunch break was from 12 to 2 pm, which was a godsend to me when I first arrived as I found the heat very trying.

Behind the kitchen was a laundry, a small tin shed with a copper and two large tin tubs with large handles. This was Nellie's preserve and it was where she kept her swag with all her possessions during the day. She brought this swag up from the camp every morning and one day I asked her why she didn't leave her things in her hut? Her reply startled me. She said if she left anything there it would be considered that she no longer wanted it, and it would be taken by anyone who found it. This puzzled me for a while, but then I worked it out. For centuries the Aborigines had been nomads and what a person couldn't carry from camp to camp was abandoned. This meant that anything left behind was treated as though discarded by the owner, and anyone picking up these goods was quite entitled to them. Simple when you work it out, but I thought it was hard on the girls to have to bring everything with them each day. The men didn't have this problem because their families stayed in the camp all day and looked after their things.

At midday I heard a strident clanging coming from somewhere amongst the buildings. 'Lunchtime', said Nat. 'Come and meet the gang'. We crossed the open space between the row of married quarters and the Big House, and went through a side gate and along the path to the original homestead which was now the overseers' and visitors' quarters. It was a huge old place set on stilts of massive tree trunks, and enormous logs formed the ceiling. The ground floor was laid with flagstones and closed in with corrugated iron. It was divided into three bedrooms and a gauzed-in dining room, and a bathroom was attached to the side of one of the bedrooms. This had a cement veranda connecting it to the opening between the dining room and the bedroom, and it had an old chip heater and a bathtub. Later I was to envy the men having hot water. The dining table was huge, made by the station carpenter from logs sawn in the station mill.

Between the kitchen and the men's dining room on the river side of the building there was a large wooden staircase rising to the upper floor. Upstairs consisted of two rooms, with the obligatory wide verandas all around. Instead of having a wooden latticework like the cottages, the veranda here was closed in with corrugated iron, and there were sections that could be swung outwards and held open with sticks. These sections were opened in good weather to allow an air flow, or bolted down during storms.

The top floor was Frank Spencer's domain. Frank was a slight, red-haired man in his early forties, with a large nose and densely freckled face and arms. His nickname amongst the men was the 'speckled hen', and he was known by this name in Xavier Herbert's novel *Capricornia*. He had a fiery temper to suit his hair, and although he kept his temper well in control you always knew when he was annoyed because he'd blush brick red with the effort to control it. No stretch of the imagination could describe Frank as handsome, but I came to know him as a very generous man who was always very good to us – nothing was ever too much trouble for him. He often gave Nat and me little gifts and he regularly brought over magazines which he must have got from Katherine. It was always Frank who gave the order for our horses to be saddled and left at our back gate whenever we decided to go riding, and if he could arrange it he made sure that one or the other, or both of us, could go with him on any trips he had to make. Because of this we were able to see quite a bit of the huge property.

I think Frank must have been a very lonely man because station protocol at this time didn't allow him to fraternise with the men, and Magnussen didn't consider him worthy of his notice. This left only us girls, and we were grateful for his friendship. He was also very good to the people who worked for him, and all the Aboriginal men seemed to respect him and always called him 'Maluka'. This was their term for 'old man', and they used this word because age is highly respected amongst them.

I'll never forget the first meals I ate at VRD. Lunch was cold salted beef with either mustard pickles, tomato sauce or Holbrooks sauce. This never varied all the time I ate in the dining room. Dinner at night was also salt meat, either made into a stew, sliced and cooked in batter (which was called 'Burdekin duck'), or boiled and served hot or cold and accompanied by either blue boiler peas or haricot beans. The highlight of the week was 'killer day' when everyone had either fresh steaks, liver or spare ribs for breakfast, still cold salted meat for lunch, but a roast dinner in the evening, with the eternal peas or beans. Sometimes we had Yorkshire pudding to break the monotony. At night there was usually a sweet dish – tinned fruit and jelly, or a steamed pudding with custard made from powdered milk. It wasn't until a few years later that tinned vegetables became available. Fresh potatoes and onions came from Adelaide in large sacks and because many were bruised and rotten from the long journey they were only available for a short time after the loading arrived.

A punkah was used to keep the dining room cool. This was a big rectangle of canvas tacked to a frame and hung from the ceiling directly over the centre of the dining table. Becky, an Aboriginal girl about ten years old, was employed to keep this swinging back and forth, and the resulting breeze was a great relief, especially during the build-up to the wet season. When Frank carved and served the meals from the head of the table he'd always leave a serve of sweets in the dishes for Becky, and she always looked forward this as I found out when we had our first overnight visitors. The cook had not expected any extra people, so although Frank himself didn't have any sweets, there was nothing left for Becky. She didn't say a word, but as Frank was not eating she knew the dishes were empty. She sat as quiet as a mouse, the punkah rate down to nearly nothing and big tears slowly running down her face. I caught sight of her sitting just outside the gauze door, my spoon halfway to my mouth, and I just couldn't take another bite. I left my plate half eaten because I knew she'd be given what I left.

This, like nothing else, brought home to me just how little the Aborigines had. Oh, they didn't go hungry! They had their own kitchen and an old white cook and his helpers, but all they were ever served was salt beef, bread, a little jam or golden syrup, and the occasional stew. Whatever food left the white staff's tables always went to the Aboriginal staff. There was no refrigeration to keep food for any length of time and the Coolgardie safes everyone used were mainly for keeping jam and sugar away from the ants and flies, and for setting jellies and custards. They also kept the tinned butter and a jug of powdered milk cool. It was never safe to keep a stew to be reheated the next day. It would usually be slowly bubbling by morning, and cold meat was also suspect. Later in the cool weather it wasn't so bad, but I'd arrived in the build-up to the wet season, the hottest and most uncomfortable time of the year.

After dinner Nat and I went back to our cottage to be greeted by Barry, a huge dog, white with a few yellow patches. He was a cross between a bull terrier and an Irish wolfhound, but looked more like an over-grown Alsatian, and I never heard him bark. He belonged to the local policeman from Timber Creek, Gordon Stott, who'd trained him to guard his wife while he was away on patrol. The Stotts had left Barry with Nat while they were away on six months' long-service leave. He was a lovely animal and I grew very fond of him, and we didn't look forward to losing him when the Stotts returned. Nat and I sat on our beds talking for a while, but as I was very tired it wasn't long before I fell asleep, and I didn't stir until the dressing bell clanged next morning.

Settling In

The next day after breakfast I followed Nat to the office where the boss awaited me. He took me to the store to show me around, and he began asking me what various items were – hammers, chisels, screwdrivers, various saws, sledge hammers, and so on. When we reached the rear doors of the store he marched me outside and down to the saw mill, then round to the blacksmith's shop, all the while pointing to various pieces of equipment and asking me to name them: 'And those?' he'd ask. 'Spoke shaves for a dray wheel,' I'd reply. Last of all, he turned and went into the saddlery shop where I named various girths, surcingles, bits, and so on. 'And this?' came the inevitable question. 'Collar and hames.' I replied. 'And these?' I looked at the small objects in his hand. I knew I'd seen them before, but what, where? I had to admit defeat. They were nose plugs for camels.

I remembered them then because once during a holiday on Wichalina station in the north of South Australia I'd seen them on a camel ridden by Sarli Mahomed. On that trip Sarli gave me a magnificent black stallion to ride for the day, an Irish Ambler. While the other horses were cantering along beside me, I sat in armchair comfort as he tirelessly ambled along. It was an experience I never forgot. This stallion was the champion racehorse of the district and regularly won the Cup each year, but mustering sheep didn't give me an excuse to try out his paces, worse luck.

'You can get to work now,' Magnussen said as he headed back to the office. I presumed that I'd passed muster and was now officially the new storeman. Not many girls would have known the names of half the things he'd asked me about, but I'd been born on a mixed farm before the days of tractors and had often gone out with the men ploughing and harvesting, as well as mustering the sheep and helping around the shearing sheds. I can remember proudly 'driving' a team of sixteen draught horses, or at least I thought I had, but looking back I realise I must have just been holding the tail end of the reins, looped correctly between my fingers as I'd been shown. Being the youngest in the family, I realise now that all the men spoilt me. I'm sure I could still harness up a full team to this day, but driving them would probably be a different matter.

Frank came with me to the store that first morning. All I could see was a mass of people, all seated cross-legged on the ground and all talking at once, with many children playing amongst the adults. At our appearance there was suddenly dead silence as they all studied the new 'kajirri' (kah-jirri, with the emphasis on the first syllable). This was the name that Nellie, our house girl, always used to address Nat and me, much to Frank's amusement. He explained that the Aborigines had no name for young unmarried women. The girls were usually married off to old men as soon as they reached puberty, and in some cases before, and the older wife or wives 'grew up' the child. This was the traditional method of ensuring that an old couple had a young person to care for them and gather their food when they could no longer do so. Conversely, a widow of middle age was often given to a young man so that when she became too old to forage for food, he and his second wife would take care of her. 'Kajirri', Frank said, was the Aboriginal term for 'old woman', and while it might seem like an insult to a European, among the Aborigines it's like 'maluka', a term of respect.

The next day at lunchtime Frank and Roley Bowry presented me with a beautiful hand-plaited leather belt and chinstrap for my hat. It was September 1st 1948, and Nat must have told them it was my twenty-third birthday, and I felt overwhelmed by their kindness. As soon as I got back to the store I climbed up to the top shelf and had a look at the hats. I had a straw hat but it could only be used around the homestead, and once it began to rain it wouldn't last long. I'd need a felt Akubra with a wide brim for riding so I found one my size and put it aside, and then looked up the price. Three pounds two shillings and six pence. Good grief! Our wages at VRD were three pounds a week and our keep. Both Nat and I had been getting ten pounds a week in Adelaide as head girls of our respective offices, but the basic wage for a married man at the time was three pounds eight shillings and six pence, so we couldn't complain. Nat and I both wanted to go to England, and we thought if we saved our money for a couple of years we could start our travels. I didn't make the trip for many years and Nat never got there at all – we both got married instead! I bought the hat anyway because I knew I'd need it and it would last for years. I made out the docket. Later Frank came in and offered to attach the chinstrap. It looked just fine and I felt I was already looking more like a 'bushie', and less like a white-skinned 'townie'.

A few days later as I was locking the store, Nat said to hurry up as Frank had some horses saddled for us. We quickly changed into our riding clothes and hurried down to our back gate. Frank had a bay for Nat and a little dark brown mare with white stockings and a blaze for me. She was a pretty buxom lass, restless and excited, tossing her head, and she looked as though she was quick on her feet. Nat mounted her horse straight away, but I had to adjust the stirrups. Frank asked how many holes I'd taken up and adjusted the other side, then he held the mare's head and gave me a leg up into the saddle. I thought he was being a bit over-protective, but of course, he'd never seen me ride and was probably just being cautious. 'All right?' asked

Frank, and at my nod he carefully let the horse's head go. Nat walked her horse quietly away from the house and I followed. Then she pushed the bay into a slow canter and I did the same, but my horse wildly flung her head up and dashed madly away. 'Ye gods!' I thought, 'A bolter!', so I hurriedly sat back in the saddle, relaxed the reins and spoke quietly to her while gently caressing her neck. Down came her head, her ears pricked, and one eye rolled back to look at me.

'Steady girl, steady now' I kept repeating, and she slowly calmed down. I felt a rush of anger: 'Who had mistreated this lovely animal?' She was so eager to please and full of go, but I found that at the first hint of leaning forward in the saddle she was off at a flat gallop. She soon settled down and I had an enjoyable ride along the bush track as far as the next gate from the home paddock. Then we turned back for home. The mare went through the same procedure, but I settled her down again and gradually eased her back into a canter. Any attempt to pull on the reins caused her to panic and throw her head in the air, which made the reins useless. When we arrived back home Frank asked how she went. 'Lovely', I replied. 'She's beautiful to ride once she settles down'. Frank grinned and said, 'You can have her as yours if you like'. 'Yes please!' I replied. 'I like her', and I vowed to myself that I would make her forget all her mishandling.

He helped us unsaddle the horses and put the saddles in the shed in our back garden. He said they were solely for our use while we were employed at the station, and he also gave us a pannikin each with a small strap attached to the handles to be fastened to a Dee behind the flaps. We found them very handy for getting a drink of water while out riding.

After a quick shower and change we were just in time for the dinner bell and at dinner Roley asked how my ride went. I told him I liked the mare very much and he told me her story. Her name was Moonlight and she'd been his favourite night horse while he was running Centre Camp. A night horse is one used for riding around a mob of cattle being held on a night camp. Depending on how many hands were available, these watches were done in shifts of two to four hours, so that everyone could get at least a little sleep. Before and after a watch the night horse was kept tied up near the rider's swag. If the cattle were disturbed and 'rushed', everyone grabbed their horse and tried to turn the leaders and make them circle, turning them in on themselves until they quietened down. This was no fun late at night and quite dangerous, and for this reason it was usual to have one of the best horses for the job.

When Roley took up saddling he'd let the previous storeman ride Moonlight. It was this man's practice to fly into the saddle, slam his spurs into her sides and tear madly off. After a few weeks of this treatment she became an unmanageable bolter. She'd fling her head up in the air and then she couldn't see where she was going, and the reins were useless. She smashed the lad into a tree and broke his arm, and when I heard this all I could think of was, 'it served him right'. Now I'd have to break her of the habit. It took me some time, but eventually I could control her with my voice alone. Moonlight was very intelligent and wonderful out mustering, and certainly knew more about the job than I did. She was the best horse I ever rode, and I grew to love her. Later she was to save me from serious injury.

Just behind our line of houses was a group of bauhinia trees, and a heap of firewood to supply all the houses with wood for their stoves. This area was the general meeting place for all the Aboriginal workers who had some time to spare. The house girls took their smoko or lunch there and were soon joined by everyone else who'd stopped work after the smoko or lunchtime bell. During my first week or so I walked past several times and every time there was a heated game of cards in progress. The gamblers sat around an old piece of blanket on the ground. There'd be a spirited round of hands slamming cards down, then suddenly someone would grab the pot. This consisted of coins, needles and cotton, safety pins, cakes of soap, plugs of tobacco and occasionally a tin of tobacco. It didn't seem to matter what the value was of the item being bet, as long as something was contributed to the pot. A couple of times I watched them for a few minutes, but could never make out what they were playing.

Frank told me later that it was their version of poker. They'd discard all the court cards from a pack and the first to obtain the amount of sixteen would win. The cards were slammed down and then swept away so fast that I was a bit suspicious about their arithmetic. Maybe it was more of who could bluff the quickest. I never saw anyone dispute any hand and I was never fast enough to add up a winning hand before it was swept away. What did it matter as long as they enjoyed themselves? These days I still see groups of Aboriginals playing cards under the trees and I wonder if it's the same old game I used to see them engrossed in all those years ago.

A 'wood boy' named Brumby had the job of keeping everyone supplied – not a very onerous task and he was usually finished by lunchtime. Later he became my 'mail boy', when I was given the job of meeting all the planes. Brumby was one of the important men in the local tribe. He was sometimes referred to as 'King Brumby', but more often I heard him called 'maluka'. This name was a sign of respect, and I sometimes heard Frank addressed the same way. Frank always dealt kindly and fairly with the Aborigines, but unfortunately many other whites treated them like animals. After I was married I often heard my husband called 'maluka', which pleased me very much. Like 'kajirri', this word has the accent on the first syllable, hence *mah*luka. This rule applied to most Aboriginal languages, unlike English which usually has the accent on the second syllable.

All the Aboriginals spoke 'pidgin' or creole when talking to the whites. After smoko one morning, Brumby came into the store and asked for an axe handle. ''Im all buggered up missus,' he said. I told him not to swear like that, but he followed me along the shelves, assuring me, 'But 'im prop'ly buggered up missus, 'im no good, pinished.' I hurriedly gave him a new handle and he left with a few worried backward looks. I sat on my chair, took a deep breath and thought about it. As far as

Brumby knew, he was using proper English. I was the one in the wrong. I just had to acknowledge that the 'pidgin' they spoke was a foreign language to them and I'd have to get used to it, and also speak it if I wanted to be understood. Presently Frank appeared with a broad grin on his face and a twinkle in his eyes. 'Everything Ok?', he asked. 'Yes,' I replied, and grinned back at him, and that was the end of the matter.

I soon learnt to speak pidgin as colourfully as the Aboriginals did to me, and thought nothing of it, though I sometimes wondered what my mother would have thought of me. She was always very particular about our grammar and always corrected us whenever we used slang, no matter how old we were. Only under the greatest provocation would mum say 'damn', and when she did that we knew she was *really* mad about something. It was the only swear word I'd ever heard until I arrived at VRD. 'Shades of mother', I thought, but when in Rome...!

My offsider in the store was Peter, a well-built Aboriginal man of about forty whose job was to fetch and carry any heavy goods for me, and to keep the store clean and tidy. He was a gentle giant and I became very fond of him, and he also seemed to be very protective of me. When any other Aboriginals came into the store he would appear at my side as if he was on guard. I suspected that after the fiasco with Brumby, Frank had given him orders to 'watch out for the missus'.

There were two others I also became fond of, a couple named Norah and Noble who worked in the Big House garden. After I'd been at the station a few weeks they stopped me one morning as I walked along the path to breakfast and asked if I'd seen their little boy, Kim, in Darwin. I told them no, and they seemed quite bewildered. I was puzzled by their reaction so I asked Frank if he knew why, and he told me that Kim, who was about eight years old and part-coloured, was one of the station children who'd been taken to Darwin to be educated. When I heard this I felt very sorry for the old couple, and wished there was something I could do to reassure them the boy was all right. I remembered reading in the *Adelaide Advertiser* shortly before I left home that the Government was taking all part-coloured children into custody to give them a good education. I thought at the time that it was cruel to take them away from their parents, but later I changed my mind. The next time I saw Norah and Noble I tried to explain that Darwin was a very big place for me to find Kim, but they seemed to have no idea of a town, and I expect I made them even more bewildered as they'd probably never seen a white mans' place bigger than a cattle station.

Nat and I arrived home from work one day to find a very excited Nellie waiting for us on the back veranda. Nellie always waited each afternoon for us to come home, and it was then we gave her any instructions about her work the next day. After we'd dismissed her, Nellie stood for a moment, hopping from one foot to the other and twisting her hands feverishly in her dress. Evidently she had something of great import to tell us. 'What is it Nellie?', Nat asked. 'My boy Charcoal, 'im bin come up sit down from Gordon Creek. 'Im my boy, Kajirri', she exclaimed excitedly. 'You come two-fella see 'im my boy Charcoal, Kajirri'.

We followed Nellie out to the back gate where a very dark-skinned Aboriginal man sat, and he quickly came to his feet. He was neatly dressed in a new set of kahki stockmen's trousers and a blue work shirt. A slash of very white teeth showed in a big broad grin and his hair was neatly plastered to his head. He was of the Jungari skin group, and while it was obvious that Nellie was very proud of her husband she'd never mentioned him before. Charcoal lived at Gordon Creek where he had his 'number one wife' and several children, but when it was time for him to go walkabout he came to spend a few weeks with Nellie, hence her excitement. I later asked Frank about Charcoal and he said he was one of the main boys at Gordon Creek, an excellent horseman and also a very good swimmer. Sometimes when the white men shot crocodiles for their skins they'd sink, and Charcoal would dive for them and bring them up to the surface. I couldn't imagine anyone doing anything so dangerous, but apparently Charcoal had no fear of these creatures.

Nat and I shook Charcoal's hand and watched the pair leave for the camp. The next day Nellie arrived smelling highly of perfume, obviously a present from her husband. I have no idea where he got it from, unless one of the white men had it sent out from Katherine. There certainly was none available in my store. I had an idea that Mrs Roden purchased such things and sold them to the Aboriginals, but it was no business of mine where they got the money from or what they spent it on. The following year it was Nellie's turn to go walkabout and she spent the time at Gordon Creek. I don't know why, but Nellie never had any children of her own. However, she was very proud of Charcoal's children from his other wives, and she considered them her 'half' children.

VRD only employed about thirty or forty Aborigines at the head station, but there was a population of 150 to 200 Aborigines in the camp at various times. This number was always fluctuating as bush Aboriginals came in to visit relatives or left again. Those without workers to claim them as family were given a weekly ration which was paid for by the Government and distributed every Monday morning. In those days none of the stations that employed Aboriginals paid them cash wages and instead, everyone employed was entitled to have his or her family kept by the station. This included parents, aunts and uncles, as well as their immediate family if they were married, or brothers and sisters if single. As everyone seemed to be related to someone who was on the payroll, this meant nearly everyone in the camp was taken care of.

During the wet season when most Aborigines in the district were on walkabout, the bush camp on the far side of the river was sometimes very large, with hordes of mangy dogs barking and fighting. As soon as the river started to rise these people made for what they called the 'Big Sunday' grounds where all their initiation rites and tribal ceremonies were held. These grounds were up in the sandstone country between Gordon Creek and Mt. Sanford, a very wild and rugged area which was never mustered. From what I could gather from the women, the area was only used at this time of the year, probably because there was an abundance of bush tucker available after the first rains and they also had their issue of dry rations to sustain them.

On ration days Aboriginals who were not employed on the station came to collect their weekly rations. Usually it was the women who did this. A book was kept with all the names of the husbands, wives and their dependants, and the amount of rations issued. This included the elderly, though most of this group preferred to eat at the Aboriginal kitchen. The women came into the store as Frank called their names. He told me the number of dependants and I would dutifully ladle out the right amounts of flour tea and sugar into the bags held out to me. Some of these bags were old flour bags, some were made from old dresses and others, usually the smaller tea bags, were patchwork. If I remember correctly the ration was six pounds of flour, two pounds of sugar and four ounces of tea per person, with children allowed half these amounts. To make this job easier, scoops had been made to hold the correct amounts for each item. I always made sure that the scoops were well heaped, instead of just rounded, to make sure that everyone received a good measure. Each adult was also given a plug of 'nicki-nicki' chewing tobacco. This smelt delightful to me, like ripe figs, but when I told Frank this he laughed and said it was the rum in it.

The Government reimbursed the stations for all the rations that were issued, and also provided for an issue of one dress or a shirt and trousers every three months, and a woollen jumper and a blanket once a year. What a day it was when it was clothing day! The men who rarely bothered with ration day all turned up on clothing day, and they always seemed to know exactly when the three monthly issue was due. Everyone was so excited to be getting new clothes that it was like a carnival. The children jumped and squealed with excitement, the crossed legs of the women sitting on the ground jigged up and down, and everywhere there were smiles. Even I was infected by the excitement and I told Peter to take down one of the ten-pound tins of boiled sweets from the top shelf and break up the solid brightly coloured mass into small pieces. I put a lump into the hand of each little kid as they came into the store to be fitted with their new clothes. The liquid dark brown eyes, usually fringed by enormously long dark lashes, sparkled and grew wide with delight. One little girl whispered ecstatically, 'Sugar bag!' 'To heck with it', I thought, 'the station won't go broke over a half a tin of sweets and nobody ever seems to want to buy them'.

When the ration parade was over or the clothing issue done, the next job was to serve a small group who had some cash to spend. A reel of cotton, a length of material, a pack of playing cards, a packet of needles or safety pins were the usual items bought. Sometimes someone asked for a tin of Log Cabin or Capstan tobacco, and cigarette papers, and occasionally one would ask for a tin of waterproof waxed vesta matches. When it was all over I was able to sit back and relax for a moment.

Then I'd get myself a pannikin of cool water from the waterbag under the office veranda next door, and start catching up with all the paperwork of the morning.

One woman I'll never forget was old Rosie, a tiny woman believed to be over 100 years old. She'd come from Queensland with the original settlers when they trecked overland with cattle and wagons in the eighteen hundreds. She'd been a teenager then, about sixteen years of age, but when I knew her she looked just like a little old witch from a child's fairytale. Indeed, all the Aboriginal children were terrified of her and ran to their mothers if they saw her coming. When she came to the store she always tried to get her hands on something she could make off with. The first day she turned up my store boy Peter hurried in from his post outside and hovered nearby, obviously to protect me. Rosie rushed at me with her claw-like, long-nailed hands outstretched, trying to frighten me, and then she asked me for everything she could think of. When I refused to give her anything she yelled and screamed until Peter shepherded her outside. Poor old thing! I didn't dare give her anything or I'd soon have half the camp begging at the store. Rosie was too old to cook for herself, but I knew she wasn't hungry because she was fed at the Aboriginal kitchen every day.

A white man in his seventies named Harry Roper ran the Aboriginal kitchen, with the help a number of Aboriginal women who did most of the work. His quarters were along side the kitchen and he rarely left them, and I never actually saw old Harry. Each week I sent the same quantity of stores up to his kitchen, but as far as I knew he never came down to the station, and lived entirely in the camp area. After I'd been there about six months the girls reported to Frank that old Harry had died in his sleep during the night. His funeral was held the next day, and he was never replaced. Frank knew the girls were quite capable of cooking and serving the meals on their own so he put them in charge of the kitchen and went up each day to issue rations from their store.

The girls weren't given the storeroom key because of the camp of bush Aboriginals who lived on the other side of the river. These people shunned the whites and only came into the main camp at night, and among them were old men who held great power over the tribe. No one dared defy them, particularly the women, and if the kitchen girls had been given the key to the store they would've been too afraid to deny these old men any rations they asked for. No doubt the girls fed these families every day anyway, but they couldn't give them dry rations to take away when they left to travel to the next group. These 'myall' families spent their lives travelling from tribe to tribe, performing the sacred ceremonies and observing the rituals. There were several different ceremonies performed throughout the year and each one had its own keeper. This meant that there were several families always circulating through the tribal area. They were entitled to receive the weekly Government ration, the same as any Aborigines who didn't work, but they never presented themselves at my store for any. Why they shunned contact with Europeans I don't know.

Other Jobs

Within a couple of weeks of arriving on VRD I was shown how to make up the mail bags for the mail planes, and this became part of my job. There were five planes calling at VRD each week. Connellan Airways' small plane did a run from Alice Springs to Katherine where it stayed overnight, and the next day it took to sweep around to VRD and back to the Alice again. Another plane did a weekly run from the Alice through the stations to Wyndham and back, and once a week MacRobertson-Miller Airways flew from Darwin to Wyndham and connected with a plane from Perth, and then returned to Darwin.

Because of its location VRD airstrip was used as a refuelling stop for all the different planes. Drums of aviation fuel and engine oil were kept in a shed on the airstrip, and part of my job was to see that Brumby rolled out a drum of fuel and made it ready for use by removing the bung. Before the planes refuelled I used a marked dipstick to record the amount of fuel in the drum. The pilot saw that the fuel nozzle was fixed correctly into the tank of the plane, and then told Brumby to start pumping. When he signalled he had enough, the pump was removed and I used the dipstick again to estimate how much fuel had been taken. Then I made out a docket for the pilot to sign and forwarded it to the fuel company which would debit the airline concerned.

I noticed that the pilots always drained a little fuel from the bottom of their tanks after filling up, and they told me this was to remove any water that might have collected in the bottom of the drums, which often were standing outside for some time. Water in the fuel line could be disastrous when they were in the air. The only oil that was ever used was for the old Avro Anson, which had to be topped up every trip on its way back to Darwin from Wyndham. The port engine always had a trail of oil running down its cowling and I often wondered why it was never fixed.

It was quite an event to meet the planes. The airstrip was across the river from the homestead and King Brumby would row me across in an old dinghy. There was an old A model Ford buckboard on the airstrip side of the river, left there for my exclusive use, and what a great little bus it was. It had once been owned by Dave Fogarty who'd driven it from Katherine to VRD many years earlier, and I called it 'Henry'. It had to be started with a crank handle and sometimes it kicked back strongly. Brumby was very wary of this and whenever it did kick back he'd give me a big grin. It ran on Avgas so perhaps that was the reason it had such a powerful kick. Brumby would carry all the mailbags and pile them into the back, and then sit posed in the seat beside me as though he was royalty. I giggled sometimes as tourists from the planes took his photograph. As soon as he saw a camera pointed at him he posed, looking into the distance like a king surveying his realm. Most people gave him two shillings for this, which he graciously accepted, but he never asked for payment.

The Avro Anson had to be started in the same manner as 'Henry', but as I was not very robust Keith Miller, the pilot, showed me how to work the switches in the cockpit while he swung the starter handle for the two engines. Once the engines started I was always a bit nervous that the plane might start off down the runway with me, but Keith assured me that he always had the brakes well engaged. He christened me 'Cockpit Annie' and the name stuck for the year that I serviced the planes.

Many of the passengers were tourists from the cooler southern states and I knew they would be finding our northern heat very trying. I'd never forgotten my experience of waiting in the hot sun at Tennant Creek on my way up to Darwin, so I asked Frank if a small bough shed could be erected at the airstrip to accommodate the passengers while the refuelling was going on. As usual he was most obliging and it soon appeared, and although it was pretty rough it did the job, and I noticed that the passengers always made full use of it. From talking to the pilots I soon learned that except for an orange or two they carried with them, the only meal they had on their runs was dinner at night. They always left at 6 am, before the hotel dining rooms were open, and they were very hungry by the time they arrived at VRD at about 10 am. Once again I had a talk with Frank and soon the station cook was supplying me with sandwiches, scones or pasties, and a large thermos of tea, much to the delight of all. After this Connellans must have made a deal with the station because a few months later they altered their schedule, and the planes stayed overnight at VRD instead of Katherine. When this happened Brumby came into his own. As soon as the passengers disembarked I'd tell them to follow Brumby down to the river. He'd row them across and become 'King' of the river as well, and his pride was evident to all. Then he'd come back for the pilot and me. Meanwhile we'd be refuelling the plane ready for the morning, and tying it down securely to cement blocks sunk into the ground in case there were any heavy winds during the night.

One day after the rains had started, Frank went across to the airstrip with me. When we got there he told me to drive Henry along the riverbank strip, which was the sandiest. At the end he showed me two large pieces of canvas which had to be displayed at each end of the strip to let the pilot know that the surface was safe for the plane to land on. We laid one piece out and then Frank told me to put my foot to the floorboards and go down to the other end of the strip. Poor 'Henry' coughed a bit, but soon we were flying down the runway. When we reached the other end Frank gave the second canvas to Brumby to lay out, and explained to me that I had to make the runway test every 'plane' day from now on, before putting out the markers. If Henry couldn't go full speed then the markers were not to be used and this would show that the strip was unsafe.

Brumby and I did this for several weeks, and then came a day of storms and high wind. We struggled down to the river which was running a banker, and I wasn't very keen about crossing over, but Brumby knew what to do. From the landing he rowed up-river for a distance, hugging the bank. Then he pointed the boat out into the current and in a few seconds we were on the other side, with very little effort on Brumby's part. I heaved a quiet sigh of relief and hoped that there were no passengers. They probably would've had a fit if they'd seen the river they'd have to cross in order to get to their beds for the night.

We struggled up the muddy bank and removed the tarpaulin cover from Henry, and were soon on our way. I raced up the strip. 'Yes! It's okay', I thought. 'No, better do one more run just to be sure.' We were halfway down the strip when Henry coughed and conked out. It was only then in the silence that I could hear the plane coming. It was unusually early. 'Quick Brumby! Run and put out the canvas back there', I yelled. I grabbed the other sheet and started to run to the other end of the runway, but the plane zoomed over our heads and landed further down the strip, then turned and taxied past us. Brumby and I took off and arrived, panting, in time to see Eddie Connellan himself and a full complement of five passengers emerging from the plane. Rather breathlessly I asked them to follow Brumby down to the river, and turned to help Eddie with the plane.

As soon as the others were out of earshot Eddie turned to me and called me every name that he could think of, most of which I'd never heard before! I stood petrified as red-haired Eddie was famous for his temper, but I finally managed to explain that the car had given up the ghost of it's own accord, not from being bogged, and he hadn't given me time to put the markers down as he was early. His reply was, 'Don't you ever do that to me again girl, I only had two minutes of petrol left.' He'd been unable to land for fuel at a previous station because of the widespread rains, and VRD was his last hope. I must have given the poor man a terrible fright, thinking he was landing on a boggy strip with a full compliment of passengers on board, and I guess I got the backlash of his relief. Brumby returned from ferrying the passengers to the overseer's quarters and then carried the overnight bags down to the boat while I helped Eddie tie the plane down. Then we all made it back to the station without any more mishaps. The next day Jim Blythe, the mechanic, went over to have a look at Henry, and he found a six-inch long centipede mangled in the carburettor. No wonder Henry had conked out! I expect that the poor centipede was only looking for a dry place out of the rain, but it could have caused a nasty accident.

Once the rains eased and the river level dropped I had to climb up and down steep banks of slippery red mud. Of course, I couldn't help but slip and slide and fall over, and I must have looked a sorry sight by the time I got to the plane that first day as my legs and arms were covered in sticky red mud. I wiped off as much as I could on a handful of leaves, but I was still a mess. Frank must have seen my plight from his veranda, or perhaps Brumby told him, because the next day I found that he'd set Brumby to lining the slippery path with bushes. It was still difficult to negotiate, but at least I no longer got covered with mud. What a kind man Frank was. He always seemed to have a weather eye out for both Natalie and me, and was very thoughtful of our welfare.

Another job I was given was reporting the weather each day. I had to learn the different types of clouds from a manual supplied by the weather bureau, and also to gauge the distance from the homestead of any thunderstorms. To do this I had to watch for a flash of lightning, then count the seconds until I heard the thunder. Every five seconds is roughly equal to one mile, so the distance to the storm was easily calculated, or so I was told. I have no idea how accurate the method was, but it was very simple to do. Twice daily I gave a report over the Flying Doctor radio to the Wyndham base, and I soon became very interested in weather reporting.

As well as my jobs of storekeeping, weather reporting and servicing the mail plane, I had to attend to the health of the Aboriginals. Usually the problem was just a headache or a cold which was easy to deal with, and occasionally someone would present with a crushed finger or a bloody wound from a fight down in the camp. Nat told me that in one particular case a girl had a finger badly mangled in a fight and Magnussen had amputated it. Nat and Mrs Magnussen had helped him and Nat had been disgusted at his callous treatment of the girl. He was one of those who treated the Aboriginals as if the were just animals with no feelings. No injury as bad as that was ever presented to me, thank goodness.

One morning a young woman with a coolamon under her arm came to see me. She was one of the Aboriginals we designated as 'myalls' because she spoke and understood very little English. Her coolamon was covered with a piece of rag, part of an old dress that had been washed so often the original colour was gone. Completely unsuspecting, I uncovered the coolamon. My breath caught in my throat and I couldn't believe my eyes! In the coolamon was a part-coloured baby girl only a few days old, struggling to breathe because her ribcage had been crushed. What had happened to her? I tried to question the mother to find out but all she could say to me was, 'baby sick'.

Just then Frank Spencer came along. He took one look and told me he'd handle it. A few minutes later he came back into the store and told me the baby was dead. He said it was a common occurrence, particularly with part-coloured girl babies. If the mother didn't want the child she would use a heavy stone from the river to crush its ribcage. The child would quickly catch pneumonia and the mother would wait until it was nearly dead before bringing it up to the office. This mother had only brought her baby up to show me that it was dying as all births and deaths on the station had to be recorded and an official notice sent to the nearest police station.

There was nothing anyone could do for these babies because the mothers made sure they were nearly dead before they brought them up.

I'm afraid that I went outside and was sick. The whole horrible episode haunted me for some time, but I never mentioned it to anyone. After my sheltered life down South I was growing up fast, and beginning to realise just how big a gulf lay between the Aboriginal and European races in their outlook towards life and death. At this time the Aboriginals still strictly adhered to their own laws and the old men of the tribes were obeyed by all. The girls often spoke to me in whispers of the dreadful things that would happen to them if they didn't do as they were told.

The End of the Stock Season

September and October were dramatic months on the station. The last supply trucks arrived from Alice Springs, and rations to last six months had to be organised and sent out to the different outstations before the rains flooded the rivers and the countryside became a quagmire. As fast as the goods arrived I had to allocate rations for each of the outstations, based on the number of people living there, and everything had to be carted out on the station truck by Frank Reid, whose nickname was 'The Loudspeaker'. You can imagine why! I also had to ensure that any mail was sent out too, because these would be the last runs that could be made before the wet set in. If any of the head stockmen needed something important or were expecting mail, they'd have to send in a 'boy' with a packhorse to pass on a message, or collect mail or other items. Otherwise they were completely cut off.

Only VRD and Montejinni had two-way radios. These were originally pedal radios but had been converted so that they could also run on battery power. There was a battery re-charger at the head station, but none at Montejinni, so the batteries there were regularly exchanged by the supply trucks from Alice Springs. These would pick up the flat batteries on the way in to VRD and replace them with fully charged ones on the return trip. When the trucks for VRD arrived at Montejinni a message was sent to VRD to advise that they were coming. This was to the supply truck's advantage as it meant that VRD always knew when to expect the next truck and could ensure they had a quick turnaround.

At the end of the dry season many of the surface waters were dry and water for a lot of the cattle came from bores. These bores had windmills, but sometimes there was no wind and because it was essential to keep the cattle watered, pumps had to be used and men had to be stationed at the bores to run the diesel engines. I was kept busy supplying them with weekly rations, but as soon as the rains arrived the cattle dispersed, chasing the showers and first green pickings, and these 'pumpers' were then brought to the homestead and given odd jobs to do. They must have thought I was a little city lass who wouldn't have a clue because it became a game amongst them to try and catch me out. They began asking me for things like left-handed hammers and saws, and even asked for striped paint, but I just laughed at them.

They were a colourful bunch with very descriptive nicknames. There was a Norwegian named 'Sailor Jack', and Nugget 'You know like' Roberts, who liberally sprinkled his sentences with these three words. He really was incredible and seemed to take ages to tell you the simplest of yarns, but he was an excellent camp cook. Another was 'Tragedy' Wilson, who got his name because calamities seemed to follow him everywhere and he always had a tale of woe to tell. Frank came into the store one day with a broad grin on his face and told me the latest 'Tragedy' story. Unlike the other men, Tragedy wasn't a pumper, but had been given the job of boundary riding the paddocks to keep the fences in order. One night he was bitten on his behind by a redback spider and it was about a week before poor Tragedy was able to sit on a horse again.

One morning Frank called in and asked if I'd like to take a run around the bores with him. I was only too pleased to have a break from the store so I rushed home to get my hat and we were soon bowling along in the ute. It was only then I woke up that I was to act as the gate opener because Frank's boy couldn't come that morning. I really didn't mind as it was a new part of the country for me – wide-open plains, patches of scrubby bush and low hillocks covered in white gravel – very different from around the homestead.

Coming around a corner we were confronted by a huge old bull standing in the shade of a few scattered spindly trees. Frank pulled up in a hurry and grabbed his ·303 rifle. One shot between the eyes and the bull was dead. I asked Frank why he'd killed it and he told me they were not marketable and were only a nuisance during a muster because they slowed the mob down and were difficult to yard. They were old scrubber bulls that had missed being mustered in their early years during the calf musters. There were so many pockets of wild rough country on VRD where cattle could flee to at the first hint of the musterers that many of them were missed. Some of the male calves grew up to be bulls and as a result there were thousands of cleanskin bulls all over VRD. Late in the year when many of the natural waters dried up, the cleanskins had to come to the bores out on the plains. This made it possible to shoot them and most of the station hands had a gun to shoot any bulls they saw.

We came across another bull and Frank asked if I wanted to try my hand with his ·303. He told me to keep the butt of the gun hard up against my shoulder because it would kick a bit. Then he knelt in front of me and told me to rest the barrel on his shoulder. This was very helpful as the gun was way too heavy for me to hold. I took aim and pulled the trigger. The loud report surprised me and goodness knows how Frank could stand it with the barrel right by his ear. I shot nine bulls with ten bullets that day, all of them between the eyes, so they wouldn't have known a thing. Not so me. The next morning I woke with a very stiff shoulder and later a lovely bruise the size of a saucer appeared, and I decided a ·303 was not for me.

A few years after this the burger meat trade to America began and bulls were worth a lot of money. They were then chased, thrown and had their horns cut off, and they were castrated to calm them down so they could be mustered and yarded more easily. The following year they were mustered again and sold for burger beef. This windfall came at a good time for the cattle industry because cattle prices were low. I'm glad I was never asked to eat one of those tough old bulls, but once the meat was minced I guess it didn't matter.

After a particularly hectic weekend when Nat, Frank and I had worked right through to get the trucks unloaded and turned around, we were given a couple of days off to compensate. Frank organised a packhorse trip to Jasper Gorge, and by taking Thursday and Friday off we had four days for our holiday. As soon as we finished work on the Wednesday Frank drove us in his ute out to a little spring, about fifteen miles from the station on the Timber Creek road. Frank's offsider, Doug, had already taken Frank's plant of horses there and set up camp for us. Doug was a very pleasant, part-coloured man in his late forties. He was married to an Aboriginal woman and had a number of mixed-blood children, but for some reason none of them was ever removed. I don't know why not, but it may have been because Doug had a special standing in the Aboriginal camp and his children were also accepted. Many years later when the Aborigines all moved to an area of their own, Doug took the name of Campbell (his European father's name) and became one of the head men of the group.

We placed a fish trap in the springs before having tea and went to bed early. It was beautiful lying in our swags beneath a stand of large gum trees, listening to the frogs and insects in full chorus. It seemed no time at all before morning came and we were woken with a cup of coffee, and toast and jam – no butter, of course, as only tinned butter was available and neither Nat nor I liked it. We soon packed up and saddled the horses, and were on our way. Doug came behind, bringing on the packhorses and spare riding horses at his own pace. Late in the afternoon we arrived at the gorge and made our way to a quiet waterhole and unsaddled our horses, then hoppled them out to graze. Frank produced three fishing lines and we were soon chasing frogs for bait. Silence reigned for a time as we tried to catch something for our dinner, otherwise we'd be eating tinned food. Suddenly my line disappeared and whatever it was I was unable to pull it in, so I yelled for Frank. He told me I certainly had a fish, but it had wound the line under some logs so I should tie the line securely and leave it. Then he suggested a walk up to the cliffs of the gorge, so off we set.

We crossed over some shallow running water and followed the high rock walls for about half a mile, and Nat and I were amazed to see tall palms growing from the sides of the cliffs. Eventually we came to a small overhang and under it we found an Aboriginal skull with a bullet hole drilled neatly in the middle of the forehead. Frank told us that in the very early days there was a large outcrop of rocks in the gorge which made it difficult for wagons to get through. Here the Aboriginals had attacked travellers on a number of occasions and several Europeans had been killed. The last time this had happened a couple of teamsters were attacked and driven off, and some of the goods were stolen. Frank thought the skull must have belonged to one of the attacking Aborigines. Later we found a cache of old rusty tins and because it was not far from where the wagons were attacked Frank said they most likely came from the wagons, and that the Aboriginals probably sat down and feasted on tinned food before disappearing back into the bush. Eventually a party was sent to dynamite the obstruction and clear the road.

When we made our way back to camp I inspected my fishing line. Lo and behold! I'd caught a whopping big catfish which we cooked on the coals and enjoyed for tea. We slept under the stars once again and I must confess I found the surroundings rather spooky that night. Perhaps finding the skull had affected me, or perhaps his ghost remained in the area. Whatever it was, the area had an eerie feeling about it.

The next day we crossed the river again and followed it along to a beautiful waterfall and rock pool. We were feeling adventurous so we climbed up beside the falls and followed the stream for some distance to where it opened out into a quiet pool. This was as far as we went and because we were hot and sticky and the water looked so inviting, we very daringly went for a swim in our underwear. After a while I felt something softly touch my leg. I looked down and saw a leech. I yelled and hastily left the water, with Natalie and Frank close behind. I've loathed leeches ever since I went swimming in the Murray River as a child and became covered with them. That time my mum rescued me and used a lighted match to get them off. I grabbed Frank's matches and struck one and held it under each leech, and they quickly fell off. Frank and Nat did the same and then we made our way back to our camp. At sunset the gorge country was beautiful, with the massive walls of rock rising beside the river turning a glorious golden red. We felt as though we were the first white people to have seen it up on top where we'd climbed, and we probably were.

The following day before breakfast we had swim in the pool by our camp – in our bathers this time – and there were no leeches. Then we rolled our swags and started for home, leaving Doug to pack up the camp and follow us in. We made it back to the springs and found a good feed of rock cod in the fish trap we'd left. They made a delicious late lunch, grilled on the coals of the fire, and it was a very tired but happy crew who finally made it back to the station that night in time to have a shower before dinner.

A few days after our trip to the gorge we had a visitor. It was always an event when travellers called into the station, especially in the early days when there were very few. Late in the afternoon a big, dusty sedan drew up at the office, just as we were knocking off work. A large lady with a very warm smile came to greet us. It was Mrs Hessie Schultz, our neighbour from Humbert River station, with her two little girls, Donna about four years old and Betty who was just two. Humbert was situated about twenty miles past Gordon Creek outstation on a track with many creeks to cross, which made it very isolated during the wet, and the only way of reaching the property then was on horseback. The Schultzes had just arrived from Queensland where they'd been visiting relatives and Hessie was anxious to get home before the roads became impassable, but as she was feeling very tired she wisely decided to stay the night before pushing on again in the morning. We helped them up to the Big House where Mrs Magnussen made them all welcome for the night, and before she left in the morning Hessie made Natalie and me promise to visit Humbert for the New Year. This was to prove quite a trip.

It seemed to be the season for visitors because shortly after seeing Hessie off another vehicle pulled in. This was driven by Wason Byers who was taking a load of wet season stores to his station, Coolibah, up the river from Timber Creek. Wason was a well-known identity, a big man with a deep, blustery voice – a larger than life figure and a real devil of a man who liked to get up to all sorts of tricks. Wherever he went there was always something happening, and he usually was the instigator. Every time he went to either Katherine or Darwin a new set of 'Wason' stories would begin to circulate. He wasn't your typical bushman because he was boisterous and talkative, but he worked hard and played just as enthusiastically. He was always a thorough gentleman where the ladies were concerned, and also very thoughtful as I discovered one day when I arrived home from work and discovered that he'd left half a case of oranges on the front veranda for Nat and me. They were the first oranges I'd seen since I'd left Adelaide and Nat said that Wason nearly always brought her some fruit on his return from trips to town. He joined us for dinner that night, but we didn't see him again as he left at daylight the next morning.

Unfortunately Wason was very hard on the Aboriginals who worked for him. A few months later Frank told us a story he'd heard from an Aboriginal who came to the station on walkabout. When Wason was out on the run rain fell at the homestead. When he returned he expected to find the rainwater tank full, and was furious to find that the house girls or some of their children had left the tap on, and there was no water in the tank at all. For punishment he made the girls strip naked and climb onto the roof where he kept them all day in the hot sun, coming out occasionally with his stock whip to make them shift to a new and hotter spot. He said it would teach them to make sure the tap was turned off next time. Later we learned that Wason was prosecuted for this by the Native Affairs Branch and given six months' jail, the first case of its kind that I remember hearing about.

One morning I hadn't been in the store for long when an impressive visitor blew in like a ship in full sail. It was Mrs Mork, the wife of the head stockman at Gordon Creek. She was a massive woman, close to six feet tall and built to proportion, and she gave me the impression that if she wanted to she could lift me out of my seat with one hand. I stayed serenely at my desk and greeted her politely. I'd heard she was an aggressive, domineering woman who ruled everyone at Gordon Creek with a rod of iron, including her husband, Fred. He was well over six feet tall with a large frame, but he was a gentle, courteous man, well liked by everyone. What he was like with the Aboriginal people in the stock camp I don't know, but his wife was very hard on the house girls she employed. All the water for this outstation's daily use had to be carried up a very steep bank from the river. The girls used a wooden yoke which fitted across the back of their necks and had a four-gallon kerosene tin suspended from each end. They had to fill half a dozen forty-four gallon drums each day, and how they managed it I don't know because I couldn't have carried one tin, let alone two.

A pair of hard, dark brown eyes bored into mine, and Mrs Mork informed me that she had diet problems and she had to have a large tin of prunes added to the rations she'd be taking back home the next day. I quietly assured her that I would add a tin to her rations and didn't bother to explain that *everyone* received a nine pound tin of prunes with their regular rations. 'Let her think she's getting a special privilege', I thought. Next she demanded several yards of calico for curtains, and I told her that only the manager or the bookkeeper could authorise the issue of materials from the store, unless she wished to pay for them herself. Without another word she surged out of the store and set off for the office. When she didn't return I presumed that her request had been refused.

Fred Mork came into the store a little later with an uneasy look on his face, and asked if his missus had been in yet. I said she had, and when I added that I'd sent her to the office about some of her requests he broke into a broad grin and with a cheerful wave he left the store. Presently, after a good look around to make sure that the coast was clear, Frank came in and took his usual perch on the counter, and I told him what had happened. 'Good for you,' he said, and then he told me real reason why Mrs Mork wanted the calico. Because of her bulk, Mrs. Mork had to make her own underwear. She made bloomers from empty flour bags, but needed calico for her petticoats. She always made the same demand of each new storeman and usually they argued with her, but I'd taken the wind out of her sails by referring her to the office. I heaved a sigh of relief – thank goodness I'd done the right thing.

When we went to dinner that night we found Fred talking to Frank in the lounge area where we always gathered to await the dinner bell. We were talking quietly when there was a call for Fred from the bathroom. Fred ignored this, but after several plaintive calls, he went to see what the old girl wanted. Ten minutes later he returned with a big grin on his face and said that his wife had got stuck in the old tin bathtub. Considering her size and that of the tub, it must have taken a considerable effort to get her out. 'Silly old cow', said Fred. 'I told her to have a shower or she'd get stuck in the tub.' Eventually Mrs Mork smilingly appeared as if nothing untoward had happened, and we all went into dinner. The next day, as soon as the truck was loaded with their stores for the wet season, they went back to Gordon Creek. We didn't see Mrs Mork again until the end of December when we passed through Gordon Creek on our way to spend the New Year with Hessie and Charlie Schultz at Humbert River station.

In the middle of this hectic end of year period the Magnussen's children completed their correspondence lessons for the year, so their father decided they could start their holidays. He asked Natalie if she would take over the bookkeeping because Johnny Roden wanted to retire and he and his wife were moving down South to be near their daughter and granddaughter. The old couple had lived on VRD for many years and had a lot of things to be packed and ready for the last trucks to take to the railhead at Alice Springs.

Johnny had an old wind-up gramophone and a complete collection of Gilbert and Sullivan operettas. For weeks before they left we were all invited to the Big House for tea every Sunday evening and provided it was not raining we listened to a selection of records. These evenings were held on the lawns underneath an enormous Indian Laburnum tree. When this tree was in flower the blossoms hung in huge in bunches like wisteria, and they fell like a lovely golden shower, a glorious sight. It was also called a cascara tree because if eaten, the long round beans had the effect of cascara, which is good for constipation. I never had to try it though, thank goodness. There were also paw-paw or papaya trees growing in the Big House garden and occasionally Frank would be given some for our table. I didn't like them very much at first, but later acquired quite a taste for them.

Another visitor was Ted Evans, the Native Affairs officer, and his junior Patrol Officer-in-training, Creed Lovegrove. After seeing the manager they came into the store and began to check what was available in the way of Aboriginal rations, and the next few days they kept the office busy, checking the Native Register and the amounts of rations and clothing the station claimed from the Government.

The first storms arrived at the end of September, dry electrical storms with thunder and lightning, but little rain, and what a sight they were! Fantastic and beautiful to watch, once I got over my fear of the awesome sight. My first experience of one of these storms was quite funny to the onlookers, if not to me. Frank had come over for a yarn as he often did in the evenings and was sitting in a rickety old deck chair while Nat and I lounged on our beds. Frank and Natalie were talking while I had my nose in a murder mystery. I'd just reached the part where the heroine saw a body floating beneath her boat when there was an almighty 'CRACK', right above my head. I thought the murderer had got me! I gave a shriek and jumped and came down to earth with a bump, and Nat and Frank roared with laughter. Lightning had flashed above the cottage and Frank knew a big thunderclap would follow, so he quickly signalled to Nat to watch me. A few seconds later came the 'bang'. They both declared they'd seen a foot of daylight between the bed and me. Believe you me, I always kept a weather eye out for lightning flashes from then on and was never caught like that again.

I've never forgotten the first tropical downpour that I was caught out in. Nat and I were soaked in half a second flat, but there was no point in changing our wet clothes for dry ones. As soon as we were out of the rain we gave ourselves a quick rub down with a towel to mop up the worst of it, and then just went on with our work because it was so warm that our clothes quickly dried on us. Besides, we'd probably soon get wet again. During these storms the ground was covered with four to six inches of running water, so Nat and I would take off our sandals and carry them under our arms. A quick wash of our feet under the nearest down pipe to get off the red mud and we'd don our sandals again, and this way at least our footwear remained dry.

One afternoon Nat and I went with Frank to Dashwood crossing on the Victoria River to check the level of the river after the first rains. There was another supply truck expected and it was a bit late in the season, but if the driver was lucky he'd get through all right. The river was still crossable, but any rains further up in the Wave Hill area could cause problems. Frank then drove us down river a mile or two to a stand of boab trees. These are most peculiar to look at. The trunks are like a large tuber with a sprout of misshapen branches at the top. They have large, grapefruit-sized seedpods which contain a mass of white material encasing a lot of black seeds. Frank told us the seeds were edible, but not very palatable. They're one of the main foods of the cockatoos and we saw a number of opened pods scattered around under the trees, but no seeds.

Not far from these trees Frank pointed out an old grave. This was the grave of the 'Fizzer,' the packhorse mailman of the early 1900s who is mentioned in the famous book 'We of the Never Never'. Frank told us the story. On one trip the Fizzer arrived at Victoria River Downs and found the manager's wife, Mrs Townsend, extremely ill. He offered to go straight back to Katherine for help, but the wet season had begun early and when he got to Dashwood Crossing the river was up. He began to swim his horse across but both he and his horse were swept downstream, and he was drowned. His body was buried where it was found and his remains were later removed to the Elsey Station Memorial Cemetery where a number of the people mentioned in 'We of the Never Never' are now buried. Mrs Townsend died long before help arrived.

From the time of the first rains I was fascinated by the wild life that seemed to appear from nowhere. A large green frog the size of a bread and butter plate appeared in our bathroom. He was so old that he was nearly white and so huge that he could only shuffle along, one leg at a time. We named him 'Fred', and Fred's favourite place was underneath the dripping cold water shower. There he'd sit, and only move aside when we came in for a shower or to clean our teeth – he obviously didn't like soap or toothpaste. He never returned after that first wet season so we presumed that he'd died of old age during the dry season.

Frogs also appeared in the 'dunny', the usual odorous outback toilet which Nellie emptied once a week. The frogs were there to dine on cockroaches that infested the toilet, and in turn snakes came to dine on the frogs. They were usually pythons, thank goodness, rather than poisonous species. The dunny was also a favourite haunt of the redback spider. These little pests hunt at night, and one had to be careful of them as their bite is very painful. When we were getting ready for bed I'd usually wait and let Natalie go to the toilet first, as I've always loathed both snakes and spiders. Frank loaned us a torch, which was uncommon in those days because batteries were not easy to get. In fact, I think it was the only one on the station for quite some time. When the batteries ran out we had to use an old kerosene hurricane lamp until more could be procured from Katherine. We always left this lamp alight all night in the kitchen, as the generator was turned off at ten o'clock and the station was in darkness until sunrise.

We were very happy one day to find that a colony of finches had decided to nest in the rafters of our back veranda and we were looking forward to seeing the nestlings, but we came home from work one afternoon to be greeted by a beaming Nellie: 'Me bin clean up that one Kajirri, 'im good tucker', she said. Nat and I stared in horror. All the nests were indeed gone and the place was spotless. We looked at one another and sighed. It was no good blaming Nellie as eggs were food to her, but we insisted that if the birds came back, she was not to touch them. She clearly thought us quite mad and went off muttering to herself with the word 'kajirri' occurring frequently in the tirade. Of course the birds never came back again, much to our sorrow. I suspect her previous white mistresses were more house-proud than we were, and wouldn't allow any birds to nest inside. Nellie had certainly been well trained. In fact we found her to be quite a treasure as she looked after us admirably, and we missed her later when she went on her annual walkabout.

Some of the other birds we took delight in were Dollar birds, Plains Turkeys and 'Twelve Apostles'. There were beautiful Rainbow birds, too. They had bright iridescent green and blue feathers, and we never tired of watching them swooping above the river, catching insects. They had long tail feathers which seemed to form an eye, so we christened them 'needle tailed kingfishers'. Another larger blue-grey bird had a call that started like a southern kookaburra, but just trailed off. I was always waiting for the laugh, but it never came. This was the Northern Blue-winged Kookaburra. There was also a bird the bushmen called the storm bird. It always appeared with the first storms and indeed, it seemed to signal the coming of the storms throughout the wet. This was the Koel, or Channel-billed Cuckoo.

Christmas and New Year, 1948-49

A few days before Christmas Frank took Natalie and me for a drive in his utility to see if we could get some wild geese for Christmas dinner. After the second gate we came to a red soil plain and Frank said that I could drive. I was just learning and was allowed to have a go when there was an open road. It had rained overnight and the ground was really wet, but there was no water lying about, so I started off. Before I could get into top gear Frank told me to slam on the brakes. Completely unsuspecting, I did, and the car spun around in two complete circles, leaving me in a state of shock. Frank and Nat had a good laugh before we continued on our way and Frank said, 'You won't forget now to never use your brakes when you're in slick mud'. How right he was!

We drove to a chain of billabongs in the bullock paddock, and what a difference a few storms had made to the country. Ground that had been bare and dry was now covered with bright green grass waving in the breeze, and the billabongs were full of water. Many of the trees and shrubs were in flower and the perfume of some of them was a delight, and I wished we'd brought a picnic basket with us to enjoy the lovely, peaceful scene. At the noise of the engine a flock of wild geese took off. We each had ·22 rifles, and spread out quietly down along the bank, leaving quite a good distance between ourselves. This was so that when any one of us fired our gun, the geese further up near someone else would not be disturbed, and those disturbed by one person might land near another. After a while the geese returned and we managed to bag half a dozen of them, enough for everyone. They were black and white Magpie Geese, and after 'hanging' in a kerosene refrigerator for a couple of days they made a delightful change from beef for our Christmas dinner.

My first Christmas dinner on VRD was unlike any I'd had before. We had Yorkshire pudding, a few fresh potatoes, and a boiled fruit pudding and custard, but there were no chocolates, sweets or nuts, and certainly no fresh vegetables to go with the goose. Nor were there any silver coins or the usual trinkets hidden in the pudding. For tea that night Frank produced some fresh fruit which he must've had sent out on the mail plane from Katherine. Nat and I had always lived in a home with a lot of fruit trees and a large vegetable garden in the back yard, so we were delighted to see it. I never realised just how much I took for granted until it suddenly wasn't there and the almost complete lack of any fresh fruit and vegetables was very hard to get used to.

It was obvious that fruit was not the only item that arrived on the mail plane from Katherine each Friday. On Saturday mornings the men who were now working about the homestead would collect their 'mail' – parcels containing bottles of OP rum. This had the highest level of alcohol per bottle then available, and usually half a dozen bottles were purchased at a time. By late afternoon loud singing would come from their quarters, which were close by our cottage, and by the evening fights would break out, usually over the Aboriginal girls. The girls were only too willing to join in for a share of the liquor, a cake of soap or tobacco, or for a few shillings, and as long as their families got their share of the handouts nobody seemed to take any notice. This had been common practice around the station for many years, and the wonder to me was that there were so few part-coloured children about the place. The only ones I'd seen were Doug Campbell's family, Griffo, a teenager I'd seen up at the stockyards, and a little girl about five years old.

The first time a drunken orgy occurred I was horrified and wanted to go straight back home. I'd never heard such language in my life! Frankly, I didn't understand most of the swear words because I'd never heard them before, and had never seen anyone the worse for drink either. One afternoon there were gunshots, but Frank soon confiscated all the guns. He told us that some years earlier the same thing had happened and someone was injured, so he collected all the guns and threw them in the river. Nearly twelve months later we were having a swim one afternoon at the end of the dry season, and we found proof of his story. The river level had dropped considerably by this time and a lot of the muddy bank was exposed. Someone pulled a piece of rusty metal from the mud – it was an old rifle barrel.

These were wild and woolly days in the North I can tell you, and I sometimes wondered just what I'd got myself into. At times Nat and I were very glad of Barry the dog's company because he would never allow anyone to come into our yard without letting us know about it. He'd come padding around the veranda and stand close to us, quietly growling deep in his throat to let us know someone was near. Everyone knew about him and they'd always call out at the gate before entering the yard. We knew none of the men would harm us, but listening to their carryings on at night was a rude awakening for me. What a little innocent I was!

That first Christmas at VRD, three of the head stockmen rode in for the celebration. One of them was 'Big Mac' from Pigeon Hole. Big Mac never did any actual mustering himself. He had two exceptionally good Aboriginal stockmen in his camp, Hector and Anzac, and they took charge of the mustering. Mac was a very good cook and always saw to it that his boys were well fed, and in this way was always able to get his quota of bullocks and a good number of branders.

The second head stockman, Jack Liddell, came in from Moolooloo. He was a tall slaphappy sort of a person and we soon christened him 'Mad Jack'. He always wore loud R.M. Williams shirts and the biggest ten gallon hat you ever saw. Later Jack had trouble with the Aboriginals at Moolooloo. He'd become too fond of one of the Aboriginal girls and her husband strongly objected, and knocked Jack unconscious. In those days it was the accepted thing that the single whites cohabited with the Aboriginal girls, and usually the girls were only too happy to oblige. In fact, one of the girls told me that most of them preferred the white men as they were always generous and kind. They gave them small gifts for their favours and because these always filtered back to their families, usually everyone was happy.

To the Aboriginals this was quite an acceptable situation. In their society, if a man came visiting from another tribe he was accommodated. What the husbands did object to was a white man monopolising their women. This either led to fights or the family would disappear one night and go walkabout. If any children eventuated the husband would 'dream' they were his and they would be accepted. In this way they also accepted some of the part-coloured children, but at this point in time they were rarely accepted into the tribe by the old men. At first I must admit I was rather horrified that such things should occur, but as Natalie and everyone else seemed to accept the situation I came to the conclusion I was being a bit straight-laced.

A few months after Jack's scuffle, word got around that he'd sent for a mail-order bride. This appeared to be true because after the calf muster, Jack went south and returned with a new wife. The poor little thing looked so bewildered as she stepped off the plane I'm sure she'd never been out of a city before in her life. Jack bustled about and insisted they be taken to Moolooloo at once, so I never saw her again. Moolooloo homestead was set on a bare dusty flat and it was one of the most primitive of the outstations. If the head station was a culture shock for her, what must she have thought of Moolooloo? They stayed there for a season, then left, and I often wondered what became of them. Years later I learned that they'd actually been married in 1947, so she wasn't a mail order bride at all and Jack had left her down South for two years!

The third head stockman to come for Christmas was George Bates from Mt. Sanford. He also was a tall rangy man standing over six feet high, and was a very good athlete. Every Boxing Day a sports competition was held at the head station and George won the footrace and the hop, skip and jump. Nat and Mrs Magnussen won the three-legged race and Nat the bag race. There were also spear throwing and boomerang throwing contests for the Aboriginals and a footrace for the girls.

Big Mac, Jack and George stayed in the visitor's quarters with Frank and ate with us, so we got to know them quite well. George took to visiting us in the evenings with Frank and we became good friends. One Sunday afternoon during the Christmas break I heard guns being fired down by the river and as I was feeling a little bored I went to investigate. I found half a dozen of the men had set up a tin can on the riverbank outside the old blacksmith's shop and were having pot shots to see who could hit it first. They were each putting in two shillings and the first to hit it took the pot each time. I was watching for a while when suddenly George asked me if I'd like to take his turn. He had a short-barrelled ·22 rifle which suited me very well, so I decided to have a go.

I asked George whether the gun shot to the left or right, or whether it shot true, and he said, 'That's how this contest started. I'd just finished aligning the gun and took a few practice shots to make sure that it was okay', and one of the men added, 'We heard the shots and came to investigate'. 'Good', I thought, 'it should be firing pretty true'. I knew that like most bushmen, George was very handy at fixing and making things. In the remote outback there were no corner stores to replace broken parts and usually no tradesman available, so you just had to make do and mend things with what you had at hand.

The men were all sitting on the dusty floor of the shed and no one was saying a word, but the grins on their faces said it all. They were ready to have a good laugh at the little lass who tended the store. This was entertainment indeed! Other than for a g'day in passing or a legitimate call to the store, these rough, good-hearted men rarely spoke to me. In those days a strict protocol was observed. It just wasn't done for a young lady in my position to speak to the men out of working hours and none of them would ever have thought to address either Nat or myself by anything but 'Miss Gurr'. They certainly wouldn't have used our Christian names – only Frank, Roley and George took this liberty. And there is no doubt that if Magnussen had appeared they'd have scattered like a covey of startled quail.

When I was a child both of my brothers had been given daisy air guns and they'd taught me and my sisters how to shoot sparrows and starlings, which were pests on the property. Because of this I was not exactly a novice – I remembered the instructions I'd been given, but this was the first real gun I'd used. The rifle had a six-shot magazine so I loaded it and cuddled the gun into my right shoulder. I took a deep breath and slowly released it, carefully sighted the target and pulled the trigger. With a sharp ping, the empty can flew back into the grassy bank and lay still. 'Yippee!', I thought. Then I looked at the stunned faces of the men and suddenly felt horribly embarrassed. I shouldn't have been there in the first place and now I'd spoilt all their fun. I hastily passed the gun back to George who wore a big grin from ear to ear. 'I'm sorry, I said, 'I never thought I'd hit it'. The men insisted that I take the pot, but I hadn't contributed to it so I refused to take the money, and hastily excused myself and hurried back to the cottage. Later George brought his gun over to the cottage and gave it to me. I called it 'Betsy' and fell in love with it. I kept it for many years and made some very good shots with it.

Roley Bowry had completed his saddlery contract at VRD and was going to work for Charlie Schultz, and it was arranged via the radio that he would take Nat and me up to Humbert River station for the New Year. On New Years eve he arrived with an Aboriginal stockman named Long Jack and several pack and riding horses, so as soon as we finished lunch we left for the Humbert. There'd been heavy rain and we were expecting the creeks to be up, but Roley assured us we'd get through. The first creek was running a banker, but Roley was prepared. While he and Long

Jack joined girths and surcingles together and strung them from trees, bank to bank, Nat and I disrobed down to our bathers which we'd put on under our riding gear. Long Jack took our clothes over on top of his hat to keep them dry, then came back and took us across one by one. We had the leather straps to hang onto, but it was rather frightening as the force of the water was so strong that it took our legs and bodies horizontally downstream, and it took all our strength to hold on and make our way hand over hand. Jack kept upstream from us, which probably broke some of the force of the water for us, but we were both glad to finally feel the ground beneath our feet on the other side.

After reloading the packhorses we pushed on to Gordon Creek. Fred and Mrs Mork gave us a welcome afternoon tea of fresh scones and cake, which was truly appreciated as we'd worked up quite an appetite. In half an hour we were on our way again. It was impossible to get across Deep Creek at the crossing so Roley guided us up the range along the wet weather packhorse track. We'd been lucky so far that it hadn't rained, but as we left the hills and came back onto the flat country, down it came. At times we were in water two feet deep and the poor horses could only plod slowly along. Other times we'd hit a boggy patch and the poor beasts floundered through. Night fell and it became pitch dark, and all we could do was pray that the rain would stop and leave it to the horses to keep to the track. They knew they were going home and wouldn't lose their way.

Hours later the rain cleared and shortly afterwards Roley said 'We're there! Come on!' He kicked his horse into a gallop and we all started whooping and hollering, 'Happy New Year!' It was 2 am on New Year's Day, 1949. A light appeared and there was Hessie, beaming with delight and kissing and hugging us, wet as we were. She said they'd waited up for us until midnight, but decided we must have changed our minds because of the rain.

Humbert River station was an unusual place as the homestead had been built from ant-bed, flagstones and bush timber. Termite mounds had been broken up and mixed with water to make a mortar in which to lay the flags, and the roof was corrugated iron with a large overhang to protect the walls from the rain. Inside the rafters were laid upon the top of the walls, so there was plenty of space for the air to circulate and this made the house quite cool. Charlie had finished off the inside walls by plastering them with an ant-bed mortar and then whitewashing them. This gave the buildings an adobe-like appearance, and he was very proud of his efforts. Hessie had furnished the place to give it a very homey atmosphere and had made the surroundings most attractive with shrubs and shade trees, She also had a vegetable garden out the back. There were very comfortable visitor's quarters close by, also made from flagstones with an ant-bed mortar, and whitewashed like the house.

Hessie bustled about and soon had a hot drink and piles of gorgeous food for us, and even cream cakes as they milked their own cows. This was unusual at this time and Charlie was the only one I ever heard of who brought wild cows with new calves to the station and broke them in for milkers. This meant they had fresh milk, cream and butter. There were a few half-wild goats about VRD so I presumed that they'd once been kept for their milk, but certainly no one milked them now. We talked and sang songs around the pianola until daylight, then fell into bed and I didn't stir until the late afternoon. We had another enormous meal that evening and sang more songs until bedtime. The next morning we started on the ride home and this turned out to be quite a tame affair – the sun was shining brightly and we perspired in the heat, so different to the cold trip up. But oh, what a glorious time it had been, and what a great start to the New Year! We talked of it long afterwards.

Before the end of the wet season a number of new employees arrived on the station. One was the new school teacher, Fay Hawson-Clarke, who was a country girl from South Australia and a good rider. This meant that there were now three unattached young ladies on the station, most unusual at that time because a governess was usually the only unmarried girl. Fay moved in with us and we soon settled down amicably together.

As well as Fay, an entire family arrived from Scotland. This was the Woods family of whom the father, Jack, was a carpenter, the elder son, Gerry, a stationmaster in training, and Alec was a teenager still at school. They came out as assisted migrants and were astounded to learn what a station was in Australia. They thought that Victoria River Downs station was a railway station in a township. There, Jack would be a carpenter and Gerry could complete his training. Jack was soon employed building new houses and it wasn't long before Gerry learnt to ride and happily went into Centre Camp. When the Morks left Gordon Creek, Gerry became head stockman there and made a good job of it. Alec joined the other children at school, and when his schooling was completed he took up his father's trade and remained on the station for several years. Jack Woods left after a couple of years, but his wife remained and went to Gordon Creek to cook for her son. A new cottage was built for them and I often wondered what the mother thought of her new home in the middle of nowhere. We saw very little of her as she seemed to prefer to keep to herself.

Another new arrival was Gordon Marshall from Sydney who came to be the improvements overseer. He was a sheep man like Magnussen, and had brought a little brown sheep dog with him. Whenever the stray goats appeared Gordon would take her out to round them up, just to keep her in practice. For a while he came over with Frank to pay us a visit, but after he arrived Frank's visits were not so frequent. At last Frank had someone else to talk to and I felt very happy for him.

I went into the office one morning and as I came in Nat turned from the wireless with a grin and told me to listen. Soon a voice began calling, giving the call sign for Montejinni, '8MN', and calling VRD which was '8RI'. I looked at Nat and we both burst out laughing. The precise voice was enunciating, 'Hate Hem Hen calling Hate Har High'. Recovering her composure, Nat answered and began the daily session. It was the head stockman's wife, Mrs Norton, giving her daily report on the condition of the roads in that area. After every wet season many of the creek crossings had to be cleared or a new crossing made, depending on what damage had been done by the heavy monsoon rains and floods. This would open the roads for the supply trucks from Alice Springs and enable them to get through with badly needed supplies. When the road was deemed to be passable a station truck was sent to Montejinni to pick up the Nortons who had decided to return to Queensland.

Some time later Nat and I went in to breakfast to find that the Norton's had arrived the previous evening. Frank introduced us to the couple and Mrs Norton proudly named the young boy and girl sitting beside their father at the table, opposite our usual seats. While Roy Norton looked proudly on she grandly announced that the little boy sitting beside her in his high chair was 'Enery'. We all got busy with our breakfasts as the work bell would soon ring. Poor Frank's face became crimson with embarrassment as our fair visitor, who was seated next to him, simpered and poured on the charm for his benefit, and all the time dropping and adding 'aitches' indiscriminately. We three girls tried to make conversation with the husband, but this proved very hard going as we only received desultory answers. We ended up talking amongst ourselves, probably much to the relief of our guest.

After a while a deep voice came from the foot of the table. 'Look to your bloody kid, woman,' said the husband. We all glanced up and there sat 'Enery', a beautific smile on his chubby little face and his porridge plate upturned on top of his head. Streams of milk and porridge were running down everywhere, dripping onto the floor, and as it came within reach of his tongue he licked it up. The mother shrieked and began berating the child who took not the slightest notice. Meanwhile, he kept the flow going by occasionally patting the upturned plate on his head. Frank gave us a wicked look, his blue eyes dancing and alight with laughter. We three girls made a lame excuse of having to give orders to our house girl before work, and bolted.

As soon as we were out of earshot we doubled up with laughter. 'Enery!', said Fay, and we were off again. We staggered back to our cottage and collapsed onto our beds, and laughed so much that the tears ran down our faces. Eventually the work bell clanged and we hastily washed our faces and reapplied our make-up, and then hurried off to our various occupations. I felt sorry for poor Mrs Norton. She was really a nice person but she tried so hard to be lady-like that she became a parody of the real thing. If she'd just been her natural self, like her husband, everything would have been all right. Frank offered to do the plane run for me that morning as I was busy in the store making up ration lists for the outstations, so I didn't see the family again.

Cold Weather Time, 1949

When the dry season finally arrived all the camps began mustering for bullocks and the tempo of the station increased. As Easter approached I had the opportunity to help with a muster in the bullock paddock. This paddock was about ten square miles and had a patch of dense scrub in the middle. When we came to the scrub I followed a cattle pad into it and hadn't gone very far when Moonlight propped and pricked her ears forward. The next minute a huge old piker bullock with massive horns came rushing towards us, and I froze. There was nowhere to go because there was dense scrub on both sides of the track, but thank goodness I was on Moonlight. As the huge creature came at us Moonlight reared and swung with it. As she came down, now facing the same way as the bullock, one of its horns scraped the saddle flap behind the calf of my leg. The next minute it was gone, and a very shaken horse and petrified girl were left behind. My first coherent thought was to get the hell out of there. We broke cover near one of the Aboriginal stockmen who gave me a broad grin and turned away. I'm sure he knew what had happened, but he must have kept quiet because nothing was ever said. I certainly never said anything because I didn't want Frank to know just how stupid and thoughtless I'd been. Mustering cattle was definitely a different kettle of fish to mustering sheep, which was all I'd done before.

By the time Easter arrived all the camps had been out mustering bullocks for about eight weeks, and they came together at Dashwood Yard, near the Dashwood Crossing on the Victoria River. There the fats and stores were cut out and handed over to drovers, the fats to go to Wyndham for the meatworks, and the stores to be taken to holding properties in Queensland where they were fattened up after their long trek. We three girls were invited to spend the Easter long weekend at the cattle camp with Frank. Magnussen also decided to take his family to camp on the river and fish, as no one had been away from the station for an outing since the rains began.

At Dashwood Crossing we found Frank had pitched his camp near some trees away from the others, and only a few minutes walk from the river. This made it easy for us to go swimming in the evenings to get rid of the dust before getting into our swags. We were all up before daylight that first morning, helping to water some of the bullocks. Each stock camp took its turn to take their bullocks down to the river crossing. The bawling of the cattle was deafening and dust rose in clouds as thousands of bullocks milled about before settling down to the business of slaking their thirst. There were always a few rogues that tried to break away from each mob, but a smart flick of a stockwhip would usually change their minds. We were soon covered in red dust and stayed that way until sundown.

After all the cattle were watered the real business started. Each camp took its turn cutting out the fats from their mob, and as the appropriate number was reached the drovers took over. Soon the first mob was on its way to the meatworks at Wyndham. As overseer it was Frank's responsibility to see that the cattle chosen were up to the required standard, so he was a very busy man, but he still managed to find time to let Nat, Fay and me try our hands at campdrafting. He pointed out the bullock he wanted drafted from the mob, then left it to us to cut it out. I soon found out just what a good campdraft horse can do for you. I rode Moonlight, and once I'd fixed my eye on a certain beast she'd take over and soon have him out on the face of the mob, with no more effort from me. There a stockman would assist me to run it over to its waiting mates and not let it cut back again, although this occasionally happened. It's a joy to watch a good campdraft horse in action and believe me, a real thrill to ride one.

At night the cattle were held on camp by two riders who continually circled around the mob. They sang as they rode, a necessity because once the cattle were bedded down for the night it was essential that no sudden sound or movement startled them, and spooked them into rushing off blindly into the dark. By singing the men ensured there was never a moment of dead silence, and the cattle knew exactly where the riders were and what they were. I'll never forget listening to the riders as they rode around the different mobs. Sometimes it was an old favourite being whistled or sung, but more often than not it was a corroboree song. Sometimes it would be both, from two sides of the mob, depending on whether the singers were black or white. It was amazing what beautiful voices some of those stockmen had, but ask them to sing around the campfire and you couldn't raise a peep out of them. Nat and Fay joined in one night with a shift from midnight to 2 am. I was supposed to do my share, but I was so bushed they couldn't wake me up. It took three days of solid hard work to split all the mobs and see the drovers on their way.

Frank had Nugget Roberts as his camp cook at Dashwood and I've never forgotten my first experience of camp cooking. Dinner the first night was a delicious roast with Yorkshire pudding, all perfectly done and with a flavour out of this world. Freshly baked bread was available every morning and that was particularly delicious too. Camp oven bread always has a lovely crisp crust all over which I particularly enjoy. Another benefit we all appreciated was that we saw very little salt beef. There were so many hungry mouths to feed that a beast was killed every day and fresh meat was always available. I think we would all have added pounds that long weekend if we hadn't ridden it all off during the day.

None of the men came near Frank's camp except for George, who was courting me, and had most of his meals with us when his work permitted. All the bushmen were unfailingly polite to us three girls, but they would never speak to us unless we spoke to them first. Even old Nugget, our camp cook, only spoke to us in reply to something we said. One day I came back to the camp early and found Nugget reading a really good book, and I discovered that he was an avid reader like me. Books were a prized commodity in the bush in those days, and later I exchanged some of mine for some of his.

The drovers who were taking their cattle from Dashwood to Queensland often had trouble with their mobs on the Murranji (Mah-ran-jeye) Track. This was the stockroute leading from the Victoria River district to Newcastle Waters, and was one of the most treacherous in Australia. A lot of the Murranji country was covered with dense lancewood and bulwaddy trees, and there were many anthills and areas of 'drummy' ground. The soil was very sandy in some parts and a fine clay dust in others, so when it rained it became a bog and in the dry season it was terribly dusty. It was what the old timers referred to as 'mongrel country'. For many years it was thought to be impassable through lack of water, but eventually water was found, first a waterhole about sixty-five miles from Newcastle Waters and known to the Aborigines as Murranji. Then the Yellow Waterholes were found another fifty miles further on, and from there it was not too far to the Armstrong River which runs into the Victoria. Once these waters were found it was a relatively simple matter to travel between the Victoria and Newcastle Waters – as long as the waterholes weren't dry. Later the Government put down nine bores which made the job of watering the cattle much easier and more reliable.

Because of the scrub the cattle would often spook at night, and if they did it was almost impossible to stop them. All the old drovers seemed to have tales to tell of the Murranji and they were always thankful to get through this part of their trip. It's certainly a dismal area to pass through. The largest anthills I've ever seen are along this road. Some of them are longer than a car and if you jumped onto the bonnet their tops were still above your head. I often wondered just how long it took the termites to build these monsters. Along the Murranji there were also a few lonely graves of drovers who lost their lives and were buried where they died.

I didn't see George on the last day. His Mt. Sanford camp and the Pigeon Hole camp had been sent to make a quick muster in the Moolooloo and Montejinni country, because the camps from these outstations had failed to bring in their quota of bullocks. The areas where the larger herds of cattle were to be found were always worked first, but even though there were plenty of cattle, some camps just couldn't get the requisite number. Sometimes this was because the head stockman was lazy, other times it was because some of them couldn't get the Aboriginals to do their job properly. The Aboriginals knew very well when they could put one over the boss, especially when the boss was lazy and expected the Aboriginals to do the work for him. In any case, a shortfall was a common occurrence and almost every year George was asked to help make up for the other camps, even though he always delivered more than his quota. I thought it was a bit hard on him and his boys, but he had the reputation of being one of the best stockmen in the North and could be relied upon to fulfil the station contracts.

By Monday afternoon the fun was all over at Dashwood and we gladly joined the boss and his family for tea on the banks of the river. They'd caught a lovely feed of fish over the weekend and it was a nice change to grill some on the coals. In the evening, replete with good food, we began a sing-song. The others must have enjoyed it too because soon we could hear the men's voices joining in from their camps. About 8 o'clock that evening we packed up and Frank took us back to the station in his utility. We were all very tired, but I think we all regretted that it was over. It had been a very special long weekend, full of hard work, but we were left with a very satisfied feeling and I'm sure any of the stockmen and drovers who were there and are still alive today would remember it as fondly.

A few weeks after the big muster at Easter, the head stockman from Centre Camp came in for supplies. He was camped at Dashwood Crossing and intended to start the calf muster after giving the men and horses a couple of days' rest. Nat and I decided to join them for a day as they were starting out on the Saturday morning. Weekends meant nothing in the bush while the mustering season was on. A day off was taken when it was convenient. Fay decided not to join us. She was a very talented artist and was painting a picture of the river to give to Nat for her birthday in a couple of week's time. She painted quite a few oils while she was at VRD.

Frank called us early next morning while it was still dark. He had our stove alight and tea and toast waiting for us, and the horses were saddled ready at our back gate. We were as quiet as we could be so as not to wake the people next door, and were soon on our way, shivering with the cold. Now that the rains were over the weather had turned very cold at night, so Nat and I wore our overcoats. Frank had attached a couple of short straps to the Dees on the back of our saddles so we could tie our coats there when the sun rose and warmed us up. We didn't have any trouble following the road, trotting and cantering alternately, then walking occasionally. The horses had a long day ahead of them so we didn't want them foundering before we reached home again.

We arrived at Dashwood just as the sun came up and were greeted with a cheer from the men. I don't think they really expected us to show up. Soon everyone was spread out and the work began. We were to muster the plains and flats down the Victoria River to Weaner yard. The old road from VRD to Katherine passed by Weaner yard, and Nat and I intended to follow it back home. As soon as the first group of cattle had been rounded up we were given the job of hazing them along quietly, with the help of an Aboriginal stockman, and any cattle the rest of the men found were added to our mob. We soon had our hands full as the size of the mob increased. I didn't ask, but I presume we were given this job so there was no chance of us becoming lost. It was hot, dusty work on the tail, but we didn't mind because it was something new and we were out riding in the bush. That was all that mattered to us, and any break in the usual routine was most welcome.

We made Weaner yard by about 2 pm and in no time the camp was set up, a killer was shot and butchered, and the skirt steak and rib bones were cooking on the campfire. These were the only cuts of meat that were edible when taken straight from a hot beast. The cook made some Johnny cakes – just plain flour, cream of tarter and bicarbonate of soda mixed with water – and cooked them on the camp shovel. With a pannikin of hot sweet tea, what a meal that was. They say that hunger is a great appetiser and believe me, with nothing to eat since 3.30 am, Nat and I were famished. Soon everyone was sleeping it off in the shade of the trees, all except those in charge of the mob feeding quietly along the river flats. Nat and I spread our saddle blankets out and were soon fast asleep, too. At four o'clock the horses were re-saddled and Nat and I helped the camp drive the mob down to the river for a drink before they were yarded for the night, ready for branding in the morning. Then we left for the long ride home.

By sundown we were well on our way home. We found the old road had been washed out in some places and in other places saplings had been laid side by side to cover sandy patches or patches of sticky clay soil where vehicles used to get bogged. When we asked Frank about it he told us that in the early days, before the Government maintained the road, branches were put down over bad sand patches and boggy clay pans, and this was called 'corduroy'. Soon it got dark and from then on we relied on the horses to keep to the road, which was invisible to us. We'd walk for a while, then trot, and occasionally have a short gallop. We arrived back at the station about 2 am, unsaddled the horses at our back gate and let them go. The boy would find them in the morning. We were two very tired girls and slept in late on Sunday. Later Frank estimated we'd done about sixty miles for the round trip. I for one never wanted to do another marathon like that. Our horses were done and had to be given a good long spell. They'd certainly earned it, and Nat and I both agreed it had been yet another memorable occasion.

Several afternoons a week Nat and Fay and I would go riding after work. It was always cooler in the late afternoons and cantering along helped to create a bit of a breeze, which was a relief after the solid heat and humidity of the day. One evening there was a full moon, and Nat got restless and cajoled me into a ride after dinner. On this occasion Fay decided to stay at home, but I eventually agreed. We set out along the road to Gordon Creek and turned off along the Pigeon Hole and Mt. Sanford road. At the river crossing the water was flowing, but not too deep for the horses. We allowed them to stop for a drink and sat for a few minutes savouring the coolness all around us. I wondered what George Bates was doing at Mt. Sanford. We'd been corresponding since Christmas and I hadn't seen him since the Easter camp at Dashwood Crossing. He was probably out calf mustering, I thought. We crossed the river and started back for home on the opposite side. It was very pleasant beneath the tall river gums and the scent of the eucalyptus leaves was a great change from the dusty road we'd been following. We cantered along for a while, enjoying the change of scenery from our usual ride through the station paddocks on the other side of the river, which were pretty bare of grass compared to this side.

It was very dark under the trees, but all went well until we neared the myalls' camp where we knew we could cross back over the river at the other end of a large waterhole. Suddenly a snarling pack of camp dogs began snapping at our horses' heels and they took off, with the dogs after us. I don't know how we managed not to hit any overhanging branches as we raced along with our heads down along the horses' necks. Aboriginal voices started screaming at the dogs and we could see dim figures racing to cut off the pack. We both breathed a sigh of relief, wondering who the strangers could be. They were probably some wild Aboriginals who always stayed on the fringe of the main camps and were usually never seen by the whites.

When we reached the lower crossing another pack of dogs from the station camp came for us. We wondered for a moment what we should do, as these dogs were in front of us. Thankfully, someone called out and we recognised the word 'kajirri', and the dogs were quickly called off, allowing us to make our way quietly home. We realised there was a large number of visitors on walkabout camped on the other side of the river with their dogs, and these dogs didn't know our smell. That weekend we heard a big corroboree down at the camp and soon afterwards all the visitors disappeared. The Aboriginals always held their ceremonies and rituals during walkabout time. We were just unlucky to have been in the wrong place at the wrong time and we decided that it was not a healthy place for any future rides.

In the middle of the dry season the mornings were often very cold and no one wanted to be first under the cold shower, so we'd stay in our warm beds as long as possible. When the first really cold night arrived, I woke up absolutely freezing. I shivered for a while, then called softly to Natalie. 'Nat are you awake? Can I get in with you? I'm freezing.' 'Yes,' was the reply, 'If you can find room. Fay's here too', so I scrambled across and climbed in beside Fay. We spent a very uncomfortable night, waking every so often to all turn over together, and we were very glad to see daylight at last. As usual, good old Frank came to our rescue and supplied us with sheets of canvas long enough to be put under our mattresses to stop the cold rising, and to fold right over our beds and cover us as well. We had no more trouble with cold nights after that. Some months later an old tin bathtub and a chip heater appeared in our bathroom, probably the ones from Frank's quarters, but the cold weather was over by then.

One Sunday afternoon Frank invited us for a swim. It was a pleasantly warm day so we changed into our costumes and went over to join him. Just down from the overseer's quarters there was an old dead tree standing in the water about fifteen feet from the bank, and a large log had been placed on the bank and secured to the old tree with chains. This made a very good platform to sit on and dive from. We'd swum there quite a few times before the rains had started the river running, but now it was back to its normal placid self.

When we arrived at the river we were surprised to find two young lads there, obviously city boys from down South. They'd come to spend their holidays at Humbert River and were waiting at VRD for someone to collect them. Frank introduced us and we soon realised he'd run out of polite conversation and had called for our help to entertain them. They seemed to think we were all country bumpkins and talked down to us all the time. It was really quite funny, so we three girls looked at one another and began to play up to them. Frank kept in the background, but by the look on his face he was thoroughly enjoying our charade.

We all entered the water and the two lads were very quiet and kept to themselves, which didn't bother us at all because we were enjoying ourselves. They could be 'standoffish' if they wished. After a while Frank began teasing Nat and Fay. I was sitting on the log taking a breather and when I caught my breath I dived in again. As I passed Frank he grabbed me by the ankle, then immediately let go again, but that was enough for me. I burst out laughing and began to sink like a stone. I moved my arms and legs but nothing seemed to happen, and I was still going down. 'I'm going to drown', I thought, and that's the last thing I remember because I blacked out.

When I didn't surface, Frank dived down to look for me. He told me afterwards that because we were swimming in the deep shade of the trees and he had to go very deep, the water was pitch dark and he couldn't see a thing. He'd almost given up hope of finding me when he felt the long strands of my hair and grabbed them. He pulled me to the surface and I came to as he carried me up the bank, draped head down over his arm. When we reached dry ground my stomach suddenly objected to its contents and water poured out of my mouth. I coughed a bit and realised that I was still in the land of the living. I must have given everyone a big fright because we were never asked to go swimming there again. Strange to say I still go swimming, but I always warn people who don't know me not to touch me while I'm in the water because for some reason I'll always sink like a stone if they do.

Natalie, Fay and I were having a quiet, lazy afternoon one Saturday when young Robin Magnussen called to invite us for a drive with his family, and he said we should bring rifles because we going shooting. When the afternoon smoko bell rang we went to the overseer's quarters to borrow Frank's gun for Nat and Fay. I would use my own. As we ate our afternoon tea we tried to guess where we were going and what we were to shoot.

The Magnussens arrived just before sundown. Mr and Mrs Magnussen and Pamela were in the front seat, so we piled into the back with Robin. Magnussen informed us that the wallabies were very thick up the river from the station and he'd decided to have some target practice. During the war the army had left two Owen sub-machine guns, two Lewis guns, twenty-four ·303 rifles and a large stock of ammunition at the homestead. These were for use in the event of a Japanese landing on the north coast. In exchange, the station supplied the army with a number of horses which were to be used by patrols equipped with battery radios to give the alert if a Japanese invasion occurred. Needless to say, the horses supplied were all the worst rogues on the station and the army men who received them had a very hard time managing them.

The army had never come back for these guns after the war. Magnussen told us he had an Owen gun he wanted to try and on the way out we four in the back seat could each have a turn with our own guns, shooting out of the back passenger side window. Then on the return run he would use the Owen gun from his window. We looked anxiously at one another. I don't think any of us were very keen on the idea of being in the vicinity of a machine gun – certainly not in the hands of someone who'd never fired one before.

Anyhow, away we went up the river. The grass lining the banks was beginning to dry off, but was still quite tall in some places, especially where it was growing under the small trees. This provided the wallabies with plenty of feed, and cover where they could duck down out of sight. We drove for some time, leaving the animals undisturbed, and there was certainly a large number of them along the river flats. It was a glorious evening. The great golden disk of the sun sinking slowly into a large bank of clouds turned them pink, red and a beautiful duck-egg blue, and the smell of the eucalypts was fragrant after the heat of the day. 'What a lovely time for a drive', I thought, but I guessed the wallabies wouldn't think so.

Eventually Magnussen stopped the car and told Fay to have a shot. She scored a hit, and at the next stop Nat moved to the window and fired, and also hit a wallaby. Everyone congratulated them except Magnussen. Young Robin then had his turn, and missed. Once again Magnussen pulled up, this time after passing several animals in plain sight, and said it was my turn. All I could see was a small head and two ears poking out from behind a patch of grass. I took careful aim and gently squeezed the trigger. Eureka! A small body leapt into the air and tumbled back down the bank. This time no one said a word and it was clear that Magnussen didn't want to be beaten by three women. He turned the car around and we travelled back to where we'd first seen some wallabies, but hadn't disturbed them. Out came the Owen gun, and Magnussen sprayed bullets back and forth along the bank. When he finished there was not a dead wallaby in sight. Nobody dared speak. He moved the car on a little further and once again the peace and quiet was shattered by the racket of the gun, with the same result. It seemed to me that the bullets were hitting the ground yards in front of the wallabies, but I didn't dare make a suggestion. 'Surely the man can see for himself', I thought.

No one said anything as we drove home. We were dropped off at the gate and politely thanked the Magnussens for the drive, and away they went. 'Whew', said Fay, 'I don't think we were supposed to beat the old boy.' 'If only he could have shot just one', moaned Nat. 'To bad,' I replied. 'Serves him right for always being so superior.' We had a good laugh as we showered and changed, ready for the bell to call us to dinner, and soon we were telling Frank and Gordon all about it, much to their amusement.

Trips around the Station

One evening at the dinner table Frank told us he had to take some stores and a message out to Big Mac at Pigeon Hole, and he asked us if we'd like to go for a trip. Unfortunately, Fay couldn't come as the children had to have their lessons, but Nat and I jumped at the chance. After breakfast the next morning Frank gave me a list of the stores needed, and when they were loaded onto his ute we set off. We were glad to have a break from our jobs and were quite excited as neither of us had ever been to Pigeon Hole. It was the usual dry season weather, a beautiful morning of bright blue skies with not the hint of a cloud to be seen. As a matter of fact, after several months of the same thing day after day I longed for a break in the monotony, with the sight of just one little white cloud. I guess one is never satisfied, even with perfection.

We left the station and were soon bowling along the road to Gordon Creek. After passing through the first gate Frank turned off to the left and in no time at all we were at the river crossing. This was the same crossing Natalie and I had used on our moonlight ride along the river some weeks before. On the other side Frank used an old dirt track which followed the river for a mile or so, then slowly turned away from the river and took a meandering route across a black soil plain.

Eventually we came to a small creek where Frank pulled up and we all walked down to see what the crossing was like. The tracks of the station ration truck showed that it'd had no trouble negotiating the ruts and holes which had been deepened by the floods, but it was obvious that the differential on Frank's ute would get stuck on the hump of ground left between the tracks. What to do? Frank went back to the vehicle and came back with a pick and shovel and started breaking down the hump in the middle, filling in the ruts on either side.

At last he was satisfied and we returned to the vehicle, but before we crossed Frank pulled his swag from the back and rolled it out in the shade of a tree for Nat and me to have a rest. I must say we were both glad to flop down and watch while he began gathering wood for a fire. Soon the billycan was boiling and he threw a handful of tealeaves in. He let it stand for a few minutes, then took hold of the billy handle and whirled it around in a big circle a few times before carefully putting it down again. Nat and I were completely mystified until he told us that this was an old bushman's trick to get the tea leaves to settle to the bottom of the billy. We got up and had a look and he was quite right – not a tealeaf was to be seen. We quickly polished off lunch and were ready to leave.

Pigeon Hole homestead was built on the banks of the Victoria River and made to the same design as the old homestead at VRD. It had the same huge tree trunks, but it was not as large overall. The downstairs part was a storeroom, and its unpaved floors were covered in dust and cobwebs festooned every nook and cranny. I doubt if the floors had been swept or the cobwebs removed for years. Big Mac obviously was not houseproud, but then he lived upstairs and probably never bothered with the rest of the place. There was not a soul in sight so Frank gave a loud cooee, and we waited. Presently giggles came from the kitchen so Frank went and spoke to the girls, but they wouldn't let Nat or me see them. We were the first white women to go there for many years, so they were too shy to show their faces. I don't think there'd ever been a married head-stockman there.

We'd arrived at Pigeon Hole in time for afternoon smoko and Frank came back with three pannikins of tea, and from his tucker box he produced a packet of biscuits. While we drank our tea we could hear some women and children having a cooling swim in a waterhole in the river. They were shouting and laughing, and making a peculiar noise in the water, almost like an explosion. We asked Frank what they were doing and he told us it was a game they played to see who could make the loudest noise.

Frank showed us how the sound was made. He formed his left hand into a tight cup with the thumb held tightly alongside the forefinger. This was to ensure that no air escaped when the hand was plunged down into the water, taking a small pocket of air with it. He held his other hand with two fingers pointing out. These were used to break the air bubble under the water, causing the explosive sound. The hand movements were an even one two, one two, left right, left right. The noise made was a regular smack-boom, smack-boom. I often tried to do this but only succeeded in producing half the sound the Aboriginals did. Years later I heard my children making the sound. They could do it perfectly, but then they had expert teachers.

Big Mac was away mustering so we unloaded the stores and Frank wrote him a note to leave with the girls. We were soon on our way home and when we arrived we found that Frank had arranged for our dinner to be left in the oven in our cottage. We were almost too tired to eat it and after a quick shower were soon in bed. It had been another very interesting day.

One of the visitors by road that year was a young policeman, John Gordon, on his way to Timber Creek to relieve Eileen and Tas Fitzer while they went on six months leave. He arrived late in the afternoon and after we all met at dinner that night, Nat, Fay and I tried to think of something to do to entertain him. Someone suggested crocodile shooting, so we borrowed Frank's ·22 rifle and the four of us set off in the dinghy I used to cross to the aerodrome. John offered to row first and Fay held the rifle on the seat in front of him. Nat was in the prow and I sat at the back with the torch. By the time John had taken us to the end of the waterhole it was fairly dark so he was given the rifle and torch. We girls then took turns to locate the crocodiles. This is done by cupping one's hands then clapping them loudly together three times. The crocodile's answer is very similar to this noise. A sort of ugh! ugh! ugh! grunt.

John shone the torch around and we could see several pairs of red eyes. Crocodiles! Slowly he raised the rifle with the torch held along the barrel, and fired. There was a splash, but he'd missed. We drifted for a short while then plunged our hands in the water again. This time Nat had a shot and the torch showed a body lying in the water. John quickly rowed alongside and while Fay held the gun and I held the torch, Nat and John manhandled the beast into the bottom of the boat, with its head by Nat's foot and its tail beside me. We were very pleased with ourselves and I played the torch along our catch, but suddenly the eyes blinked and the tail quivered. Nat and Fay hastily put their feet up on the seats, Fay dropped the rifle and I dropped the torch, and I can still recall verbatim the ensuing conversation: 'Swim for the shore,' yelled Fay, 'shoot it, shoot it,' yelled Nat, 'and sink the bloody boat?' said John. I was speechless! There we were in the middle of the river in the pitch dark, with a live crocodile on board!

Natalie's shot had only creased it. John leaned forward, grabbed the crocodile's tail and sternly ordered me to hang on to it as tightly as I could. I sat there, paralysed, with the tail draped over my shoulder and praying it would not start to struggle. I knew that if it did I had no hope of holding it because crocodiles have particularly strong tails. Next John grabbed the jaws with both hands and clamped them tightly together, and ordered Nat to tie the painter, the short rope used for tying up the boat, around its jaws. When this was done he took the tail from me and I fished the torch up from the bottom of the boat so we could at least see once again.

John soon had the crocodile tied nose to tail in the bottom of the boat and then he took up the oars and rowed madly for the landing about five minutes away. We got there with no further mishaps and I'd never been so glad to stand on dry land. Frank was there to see how we'd fared, and he and John soon hauled the poor beast out onto the bank and despatched it with a bullet between the eyes. The next day Frank had it skinned and promised to have it tanned for Nat. The carcase was taken by the Aboriginals and I'm sure there was a great feast down in the camp that night. It was a freshwater or Johnstone River crocodile, six feet eight inches long, longer than the dinghy we'd been in. The next day I overheard John telling one of the men that it was the first and last time he went shooting with a bunch of bloody females. I had a quiet chuckle.

John returned to VRD a few months later during his first horse patrol of the district – there were no police vehicles in the bush in those days. There was a calf muster on that weekend so John joined us and we all went out and camped at Centre Camp in order to make an early start. The dry season days are so hot that all animals feed in the cool of the morning and early evening, and if you wanted a good muster you had to be out before dawn to catch the cattle feeding on the open plains. Once they went back into the scrub you'd lose half of them. That night we went to bed fully clothed, except for our boots, and it was still dark when we were roused from our swags the next morning. A quick wash in a dish of icy cold water got the sleep out of our eyes and woke us up very smartly. Then we all made a beeline for the cook's fire to try and warm ourselves up, but we made sure we didn't get in his way. Camp cooks are a funny breed and can take umbrage at the smallest thing. No one ever dares to upset them, especially first thing in the morning. As soon as the billy boiled we were each given a big pannikin of lovely hot coffee, which was a good hand warmer.

After a breakfast of steak and freshly baked bread we were on our way, just as the first streaks of dawn were lighting the sky. The usual ground mist which always seemed to roll across the land in advance of the rising sun was like a cold wet blanket to ride through. My teeth were soon chattering, but I consoled myself with the thought that chasing a few cattle would soon warm me up, and it wasn't too long before the muster was in full swing. We came out of the scrub before the cattle were aware of us so it wasn't too difficult to block them from escaping, and we soon had a good mob, with more being added as each group of riders hazed their tally towards us. The whole operation went like clockwork and we moved the cattle towards the nearest yards to brand the cleanskins.

We were nearly through mustering when a riderless horse shot past me. It was John's horse so I took off after it and caught hold of the flying reins, and after a struggle managed to pull it up. Both horses were plunging about as the runaway fought to get free, and their reins soon ended up tangled together. At last they stood, mine quietly but the other with eyes rolling in fear. It was a horse that John had recently broken in and it was still half wild. Thankfully, John came up and proceeded to untangle the mess. My hand was so tightly tied up in his reins I couldn't let go. To my surprise, instead of remounting his horse he led it away on foot. He was looking for a soft patch and when we came to some sand by the creek John mounted his horse again. He no sooner hit the saddle than the horse bucked and off he went into the sand. This procedure was repeated a couple of times and at the third attempt the horse danced skittishly for a bit before settling down, and we rode quietly back to camp. That horse was definitely 'green' and would take a few more weeks of daily handling before it settled down into a well-broken in animal.

That man sure had guts! Most men would have given a horse like this to an Aboriginal offsider to ride, but not John. He knew he was going to be bucked off so he found the best spot for it to happen, and he persevered until he stayed on. I got to know him well over the years and found him a friendly, humorous man who would never admit defeat. He didn't mind telling stories about himself if the joke was on him, and he could tell some good yarns, too. John told us he would sometimes sit cross-legged on the police station veranda listening to the ABC Play School of the

Air. To break the monotony John would go through all the actions the children were told to do. There wasn't another white person to talk to for a hundred miles around and it was a way to relieve the boredom of being on his own, but can you imagine a big burly policeman doing this?

In July 1949 there was great excitement because Magnussen had decided to hold a race meeting, the first one on VRD for many years. Frank and Gordon were busy for weeks with all the Centre Camp boys building a track and bough shelters, and just before the great day all the outstations came in, each bringing a string of their best horses. These had to be grass fed because horses fed on oats had more stamina, and only Humbert River and the head station could get oats. Charlie and Hessie Schultz came in from Humbert River and set up their camp down at the crossing, close to the racetrack. We visited them there and as usual Hessie had a feast of goodies she'd baked for the occasion, and their camp became a very popular port of call. Humbert was way off the main road and never had any through traffic, and it didn't have an airstrip. All their mail was delivered to VRD and a boy with packhorses was regularly sent to collect it. Hessie was a very good cook and delighted in entertaining people, so I guess her life was a pretty lonely one.

George Bates was one of the first to arrive. He had several horses for me to ride, and Frank and Centre Camp supplied Natalie and Fay with mounts for the big occasion. There were to be three ladies' races and three men's races, with a novelty event to finish off the day which was open to everyone, and of course, a 'blackfellow's race'. As the great day dawned, people seemed to come from everywhere. Several planes came from Darwin, Alice Springs and Katherine, and among the passengers were two bookmakers. It was marvellous to me how people found out about events like this being held way out in the bush. A lot of cars and trucks also turned up so there was quite a tent city down by the river. Frank's quarters were soon full with the other head stockmen, but George camped down with his horses to keep an eye on them. Nat, Fay and I stayed in our cottage each night, but I still saw quite a lot of George because he had most of his meals with us, and he and I soon became what people today call an 'item'. I received a bit of teasing from my friends and I think George did, too.

Would you believe it – George won all three men's races and I won all the ladies' races! Finally the last race began and it was a walk, trot and gallop. George was soon in the lead, with me not far behind. My horse had a very quiet temperament, but George's was a bit flighty, and near the end of the walk section his horse broke its stride and he had to go back and start again. I romped home amid loud cheers from my backers. This made me the champion jockey of the meet, but I felt that things had been a bit one-sided. Mt. Sanford was beautiful horse country so the station stallion was kept there and all the VRD horses were bred there. This meant that each year George had the first pick of the horse muster and he was a very good judge of horseflesh.

That night everyone donned their 'glad rags' and we danced under a large bough shed until well into the morning. The music came from an old gramophone and the floor was of earth, so after an hour or so of enthusiastic dancing there was a terrific dust cloud rising from under our feet. A few of the men began a two-up game behind the dance area, but they were soon discovered by two visiting police officers who quickly put a stop to it. The tale later got around that it was just as well because the instigator and his mate were running a racket, and all the locals would have lost their money. They were quietly told to leave, or else. By morning everyone was covered with thick dust to their knees, but nobody cared. Most of the women wore special dresses flown up from Perth for the occasion, but after that night I think they all went into the ragbag – I know that I gave mine to Nellie. There must have been some sore heads the next morning, but everyone was given the day off and like us, they all slept in.

That first year the prizes were made up from the entrance fees and not worth much, but in later years they were mostly donated and some were worth quite a bit of money. Because the horses I won on were George's he collected the prize money, but I proudly received the premier jockey's whip and was dubbed the 'Darby Munro' of the meeting. The meeting in 1950 was a much bigger affair. As well as Humbert River, Wave Hill station came in with some good horses, and the Fogarty family arrived on their way through to Auvergne station. The eldest of the Fogarty boys was Lloyd and he had his wife Camille and their small daughter with him, and their daughter was a bit fretful. By this time I was married and had a baby daughter myself, so we put the two of them together in my daughter's large meat-safe cot. Shortly after the races my baby developed measles, so then I knew what had been the matter with the Fogarty's girl.

In later years the racing men began to get serious about their horses, and the rules were changed to allow feeding with oats. In about 1956 or '57 the racetrack was shifted to where the aerodrome was later built, and a cement dance floor was laid down with bales of hay scattered about for seats. A few empty forty-four gallon drums were placed at strategic places and fires burnt in them all night to keep out the cold. Charlie Schultz bought good horses and soon began winning his share of races, but I don't think any of the later meets quite compared with that first truly 'bush' meeting, where all comers had just their ordinary grass-fed nags running for a bit of fun.

Marriage – September 1949

One Friday morning when we went for our breakfast we found that George had ridden in overnight from Mt. Sanford, quite a feat as it was a journey of about sixty miles. When he arrived at VRD he let his horse go in the station spelling paddock and arranged with Frank to get another one for the return ride. He'd come in to report that all the Aborigines at Mt. Sanford had run away, and he and Nat spent quite some time with Magnussen in his office, contacting the Wave Hill police to try and get them back again.

While he was in, George applied for leave. He hadn't been off VRD for several years so had decided it was time for a holiday, and was planning to visit his mother and sister in Barcaldine. His father had been the outback mailman in the Aramac–Hughenden area for many years and that's where George had been born. He also planned to go on to Sydney to see his father who'd retired there, and to meet various aunts, uncles and cousins that he'd never met before. Permission was granted for him to take six weeks' leave after he finished the mustering.

Over the weekend George asked me to marry him. I was flabbergasted and didn't know what to say. We hadn't so much as exchanged a kiss at this point, but in a panic I said yes, thinking that I could send him a letter later and call it off. We decided that he could buy a ring when he was in Sydney, and spent some time looking at an Angus and Coote catalogue that George borrowed from someone. I chose a sapphire, which was my birthstone.

A few weeks after George returned to Mt. Sanford and before I'd written to him to call the engagement off, Mrs Magnussen stopped me and asked if September 20th would be suitable for my wedding date. She said that Natalie was to be my bridesmaid and her daughter Pam my flower girl. She'd ordered the material for their dresses and was going to make them herself. I was shocked, but couldn't think what to do or say. I didn't want to marry George at all, but I was afraid that if I called it off now I'd more than likely be given the sack and felt I had no choice but to go along with it. Mrs Magnussen also told me that her husband was to give me away! 'Oh no!' I thought. He was the last person I would have wanted. I would've preferred Frank Spencer if I'd been given a choice. Apparently everything for the wedding was already arranged between the Magnussens and Natalie, and I felt as if I was just a puppet. After I got over the shock I wondered why Mrs Magnussen had even bothered to ask about the date because I hadn't been asked about anything else. Later when I menstruated I finally worked that one out for myself.

George left for his holiday a month later and I began to receive his letters, and several weeks later a registered parcel came through the post from the jewellers. Included with the engagement ring was a matching eternity ring and a wedding ring, both of which I put away, but I began wearing the engagement ring. I have no idea who told George, but a letter arrived from him with his birth certificate enclosed and asking me to make all the arrangements with the minister. It suddenly hit me that I was to be married in less than three months time, so I asked Magnussen for permission to go to Adelaide to choose the material for my wedding dress, and to buy my trousseau. He gave me time off to do this and I went down to Adelaide for a couple of weeks. I should have called it off from there but by this time the wedding had a life of its own and everyone was involved. I just didn't have the self-confidence to do it.

In Adelaide a dear friend offered to make my dress for me, and as Nat and Pam had chosen blue-figured organdie I chose the same in white. I spent a few hectic weeks gathering all that I'd need to get set up in my new home, and friends and family gave me many lovely wedding gifts, some ornamental but mostly practical things. At the last minute I took my mother's advice and bought a sewing machine. It served me faithfully for nearly forty years before I traded it for an electric model. I also purchased a large metal travelling trunk to carry my new things and my mother assured me that it would be sent on for me. She also packed many of my old things in a large old wooden tea-chest which had belonged to my grandmother.

Unbeknown to me my mother included two sets of china, one her best bone china tea set which had been one of her own wedding presents, and the other that a cousin who'd lived in China for many years had given her. The cups of the set from the cousin were so delicate that when you held them up to the light they were almost transparent. I'd always loved them, but unfortunately, when the boxes and trunk arrived they were badly damaged. They'd been placed on top of the supply truck from Alice Springs and had been hit by tree branches. The steel trunk had one corner caved in and one side of the tea chest was also damaged. Much to my horror, all the Chinese cups were completely shattered. Most of the cups of my mother's tea set were also lost and the milk jug was cracked. When I found them I just sat and cried, but I didn't tell mum what had happened to her treasures. The sewing machine was damaged, too, but the station mechanic welded it together and got it working again.

In Darwin on my way back to VRD I called in to see the minister at Darwin's Christ Church Cathedral. I'd collected my birth certificate from my mother in Adelaide and with George's in hand I was able to make all the arrangements. I was taken in to see the church and I was surprised to see that, just like the house at

Humbert River, the eves were not closed in. The rafters sat on top of the walls and air could flow into the room from outside to help keep it cool in the hot weather. What amused me was to see a number of small finches flying in and out to their nests up in the rafters. I hoped that they'd behave themselves on my great day, and not disgrace themselves as they flew over the congregation.

As the big day neared the Magnussen's decided to drive to Darwin and Natalie, Fay and I were invited to go with them. It was rather a tight squeeze in the back for Robin and we three girls, but we managed. Fay had decided to return to Adelaide and was going to catch a plane south after the wedding. My mother and my sister Gwenda with her little three year old son flew up from Adelaide, and for 'something old' to wear mum gave me an antique brooch which had belonged to my great grandmother. I treasure it to this day.

George and I were married in Darwin on September 20th 1949. The reception was held on the lawns outside the Hotel Darwin, a beautiful spot beside the harbour with a cool breeze blowing off the water, and much cooler than being inside on a hot tropical night before the days of air conditioners. I guess no one ever forgets their wedding night. In our case all the wedding guests were staying at the Darwin Hotel so George and I decided to spend our first night at the Sea Breeze Hotel at Nightcliff. We left the reception and drove out along Bagot Road until the bitumen stopped and then followed a winding dirt track through the scrub, with bushes brushing against the sides of the taxi. Eventually we arrived and were shown to our hut by hurricane lamp. In those days the Sea Breeze Hotel was an old Sydney Williams hut which housed the bar, dining room, kitchen and office. The guests' accommodation in the surrounding jungle was series of old wooden army huts that had been used during the war by men manning gun emplacements along the foreshore. Not far from our hut there was the remains of one of these, covered in vines and creepers. The huts had one room and two single beds with mosquito nets, and across the back of each was an alcove containing a shower and toilet.

About 2 am I woke up and needed to go to the toilet – I wasn't used to so much wine. I very carefully eased myself out of bed so as not to wake George, and felt about for a torch we'd been given. I couldn't find it, so I crept to the toilet in the pitch dark, feeling my way. I sat down. Next minute I rose with an unearthly shriek as something wet, cold and slimy hit me on the bottom. What an uproar! People came from every direction, torches and hurricane lamps bobbing, to be met at our door by a sheepish George with the words, 'It's only a green frog in the toilet.' So much for the quiet newlyweds blending into the background! I can tell you I ate a very quick breakfast next morning and was glad to get away from the place and start on our honeymoon.

We caught the bus to Mataranka and after two delightful weeks spent at the hot springs tourist resort, we went in to Katherine to catch Connellan's plane home. This went via Timber Creek where we found Tas and Eileen Fitzer had just returned from their long service leave. I've never liked little planes and always seem to get sick in them. I became horribly sick on this plane and at Timber Creek Eileen, who was a nurse, insisted that I be off-loaded. After a few days John Gordon drove me over to VRD where I was told I'd missed a terrific welcome home party. Mr and Mrs Magnussen had invited my mother to spend a few weeks on the station after the wedding, so George had gone on to Mt. Sanford to get the house ready for the three of us. The plan was that when Alf Absolom came to service the bores around Mt. Sanford he'd take her on to Wave Hill where she'd catch a plane back to VRD and on to Darwin. This would be much better for her than going back to VRD by truck over the very rough sixty miles.

When I'd become engaged a new girl had to be employed to learn my job. She arrived a few weeks before the wedding and turned out to be Dorothy Coleman, a very attractive blonde English girl with a peaches-and-cream complexion and a very strong accent. She'd just arrived from the old country and was a lovely girl, full of fun, and one who didn't mind when we laughed at her mistakes. She was also very quick-witted and often had us in fits of laughter with her tales of her time in the army during the Second World War.

One Sunday afternoon while we were having afternoon tea the men in their dining room just outside our window began to argue. They were all full of rum and it looked as if there would soon be a free-for-all. Frank pushed his chair back and was about to go in to try and cool things down when the cook's alarm clock went off in the kitchen. Instantly all was quiet, and into this silence came Dorothy's clear English voice, 'End of round one!' There were loud guffaws from the men and we were all convulsed with laughter. With a broad grin Frank sat down again, and because the men realised we could hear everything they were saying when they raised their voices there was only a quiet murmur from then on.

All the men had a great deal of fun with Dorothy. Never a day went by without one or two of them coming in for various items, supposedly to do with their work. I can't tell you the number of times she'd go looking along the shelves for left handed tools of all descriptions, until I'd call out, 'Oh, Dorothy!' She'd come back with a good-natured smile on her face and exclaim, 'Oh! You men!', and with a broad grin they'd be on their way. One day a bright spark asked for a can of striped paint. Dorothy collected the key to the paint store and went off while her customer made himself comfortable on the counter and prepared for a good 'chinwag' with me. Dorothy eventually returned, covered with dust and cobwebs, and declared that she'd looked through all the store of paints – no mean feat – but there was no striped paint. He gave me a broad wink and said he'd have to mix some for himself, and left. He'd have a really good tale to tell his mates this time and I didn't have the heart to tell her she'd been had once again.

When I returned from my honeymoon mum and I had to wait at VRD for a couple of weeks before a truck could take us to Mt. Sanford and Magnussen asked if I would write up all the store books. I was only too pleased to have something to do so one morning I went into the store, opened up the ledgers, and proceeded to enter the invoices and price the goods. I reached my hand down for the cart-notes that were always left hanging on nails at the side of the store desk, but couldn't find them. These notes recorded the date of arrival of each trucks, the weight of each case or carton and the number of jars or tins in each. This enabled the cost of the freight on each item in the case to be calculated on the tonnage paid for each truckload.

I leaned over to see how I could have missed them and there was nothing there – just the bare nails. Dorothy saw me peering about and told me that she didn't like the look of those untidy papers so she'd thrown them all out when I'd left to get married! I was struck dumb! I distinctly remembered telling her just what they were for before I handed over the store. I tried to explain just how important they were, but it didn't sink in – she just brushed my explanation aside. Oh well! If she wasn't concerned, why should I be? The store was now her responsibility and she could run it her way. I entered all the invoices and left all the freight charges for her to calculate later. I didn't have time to try and sort the papers that were held in the office. The cart-notes there would not be matched with the invoices as I'd kept them in the store. I wonder just how she got on.

While waiting to go to Sanford I stayed in my old cottage with Nat, and one evening just as we were thinking of going to bed Barry suddenly started to growl low in his throat, and we knew that there was someone outside. Then a voice called out and we went to the front door to see who it could be at this hour. It was one of the stockmen, Joe Zagami. He stood there holding a blood-soaked handkerchief to his face and asked us if we could do anything for him as he was in a lot of pain. He'd gone to Magnussen that afternoon and asked if he could take the next plane to Katherine as he had a toothache. Magnussen told him that there was no need as he'd pull the tooth himself. He then proceeded to do so, and left Joe with terrible bleeding.

Neither Natalie nor Fay seemed to know what to do, but I thought the best thing was to poultice his jaw to try and give him some relief from the pain. I went into the kitchen and built up the fire once again, and put all the salt we had into a baking dish and placed it into the oven. Fay asked me what it was for and I explained that my sister Margaret once used a needle to prick a pimple on her face and it festered badly. Her friend Jo who was a nursing sister had helped her by doing what I was about to do – put hot salt packs on her face until the swelling went down. I collected some cloths and made up several salt packs, and sat up for the next few hours reheating the packs in the oven as each one became cold. Eventually Joe said the pain had eased considerably and he felt much better, and he probably realised I was dead on my feet because he thanked me very much and told me to go to bed. He said he'd change the packs himself until he thought he could get some sleep. Joe was gone when we got up the next morning. He caught the next plane to Katherine and at the Katherine Hospital he was told he'd been given an overdose of anaesthetic when his tooth was drawn. When the next medical plane made a visit some items were removed from the medicine chest. 'Not before time', we girls thought.

After some weeks the house at Mt. Sanford was ready – as ready as possible under the circumstances. My mother and I were picked up by a station truck and I set out to begin a new life on one of the remotest outstations in Australia.

Into Isolation

My first sight of Mt. Sanford wasn't encouraging. The buildings were on the edge of a small plain and the house was the usual one-roomed corrugated iron building with wide verandas on all sides and a concrete floor. A bathroom was attached and this had just a cold-water tap and shower, and it was freezing to take a shower in the cold weather. One small river gum and a few bloodwood trees were about the only greenery in the yard, and two nutwood trees stood at the entrance to the vegetable garden. Down by the creek there was a lot of pandanus, and plantains or cooking bananas grew in the overflow from the water tank. Further up the creek there were some large trees and the view from the back of the homestead was of rocky hills covered in spinifex, with a few stunted trees here and there.

Twenty yards away stood the original homestead, a single room built of big logs with a veranda all around and a floor of flagstones set in ant bed. It was now used as a store and kept locked, and the veranda was where the men camped when the stock camp was in. The ant-bed made the place very dusty and each morning after sweeping, the house girls would sprinkle the floor with water to settle the red dust. Thank goodness my house had a new concrete floor! The old building was similar to the top floor of the overseers' quarters at VRD and also the house at Pigeon Hole in that the veranda was closed in with corrugated iron and it had similar prop-out windows, but here the window sills were lower, about a foot and a half from the floor, and this allowed a flow of air over the men's beds. One back corner of the veranda was fly-wired and used as a dining room, and this connected with the kitchen which was built onto the back. Here Dave Galton, the cook, reigned.

Magnussen had told me that because I was a head stockman's wife I could tell the cook to make anything I liked for our meals, but I had the sense to know that Dave knew more about his job than I did so we just ate whatever he cooked for us, and very good meals they were too. Dave had an excellent vegetable garden where he supervised three girls every afternoon, and the resulting vegetables and paw-paws were a delight. There were tomatoes, cucumbers and lettuce with our cold salt meat, and an even wider variety for dinner at night. 'Why', I wondered, 'didn't they have a garden at VRD?'

Years later I met an old Katherine identity, Mrs Shaw. She was the matriarch of the Fogarty family and when she heard that I'd lived at Mt. Sanford she told me that she'd been the first white woman to ever live there, and to her knowledge I was the second. Of course, she never had the benefit of the new iron house that I had. She and her family had lived in the old original house so her lot must have been far worse than mine in those early days. She really was a great old pioneer woman of the outback and became a great friend of mine.

While we were being married and on our honeymoon the goods I'd bought in Adelaide were coming up on a truck. These hadn't arrived yet and there was absolutely nothing at Mt. Sanford except a few homemade beds. Fortunately the Magnussens had decided to refurnish the Big House and they sent over their old furniture. Goodness knows what we'd have done otherwise. A carpenter was sent up to make a gauze dining room at one side of the house and when I put the Magnussens' old dining table, chairs and sideboard in they looked very grand, but I soon found out why they'd given the double bed away. It was a horror. The springs had collapsed and after sleeping on it that first night I woke up with a very sore back. I persuaded George to do something about it, and he found some old packing case boards and nailed them to the bed frame. It was certainly solid to sleep on, but a definite improvement on the springs.

Mum slept on the back veranda on one of the homemade bushmen's beds, which she said was very comfortable. This was made from bush timber and consisted of four roughly dressed corner posts about six inch square and thirty inches long, and joined together with very solid squared rails. These rails were drilled every two inches with a large auger bit and through these holes long strips of greenhide were laced and interwoven from side to side. This made a very strong base with just enough give in it to be comfortable. On this was placed a mattress of sacking or ticking filled with dry spinifex grass.

After we arrived mum and I spent our time unpacking all my wedding presents. I carefully placed my crystal glasses and china in the sideboard, and locked the door because I didn't trust the house girls to handle them. I guess my mother must have noticed the absence of the cups, but she didn't say anything. Eventually Alf Absolom arrived to service our windmill and the one at Black Gin bore, and he took my mother to Wave Hill, as planned. She had to wait there for several days for the plane to arrive so she asked for something to do, and later she told me she was very amused when she was given a pile of men's socks to mend. The manager's wife commented that she hated darning and mum replied that she did too, but it was better than sitting idle.

When mum left, George set to work making canvas blinds for the bedroom side of our house. Then he made a bough shed across the front and I planted creepers on this to screen it further, and hung four beautiful baskets of Wandering Jew which I'd bought from Mrs Roden before she left the station. They were magnificent, ivy-like plants with trails almost six feet long. On our front veranda I had all my books in a bookshelf made from packing cases, and also our pride and joy – two squatter's chairs. These were wooden with canvas seats, and the side arms extended out far enough to rest your legs on them. They were very comfortable and in the years to come I was to spend many a relaxing hour there with my nose in a book.

Extending from the bathroom at the back George built a leaning shade from logs covered with chicken wire and thatched with spinifex grass. These extensions made the whole house considerably cooler and after my house girl had hosed the place out each afternoon it was very pleasant to have afternoon tea on the front veranda.

Water was often a problem at cattle station homesteads and outstations in the early days. I've mentioned how the girls at Gordon Creek had to carry buckets of water from the river on yokes and fill a number of forty-four gallon drums each day. The same system was used at Pigeon Hole, but at Mt. Sanford we were lucky in that right at the house we had a windmill with a large tank on a stand, and there was always plenty of wind to keep this filled. The only trouble I can remember was during one wet season when a pump rod broke and George had to pull the bore and fix it himself. Being the wet season there was no white staff to help, so guess who did? George attached a cable to the rods and fixed the other end to our car. Then I had to drive the car backwards and forwards very slowly, first to pull up the pump rods and then to return them after George had replaced a broken washer.

There were only three taps from the tank. One was in our bathroom and another in the men's bathroom, which was just a small cubicle made of corrugated iron and with a hessian curtain for the entrance. It was open to the sky and stood on its own in the back yard near the laundry shed. The third tap was placed at the back door of the kitchen. From this tap the girls had to carry buckets of water to use in the kitchen and to clean the men's quarters, and it was also used to water the garden.

On the side where we slept George carted in a lot of soil and goat manure to make a patch of couch grass lawn for me. This was watered by the run-off from the bathroom and I soon decided I'd make a garden there as well. It took a lot of work because the station was built on a limestone ridge, but I didn't have much else to do so I slaved away with a pick and shovel, and occasionally a crowbar, to remove the larger rocks. Eventually I had eight circular beds, and got the girls to cart soil from the creek beds and manure from the goat yard to improve what little soil was left after all the stones were removed. I then planted banana palms and watermelon seeds, and I had a hose sent up with the next lot of supplies. I fitted it to the bathroom tap and did the watering myself. That first year I grew the biggest watermelons you ever saw, but by the time they were ready to be picked I was away in Adelaide awaiting my first child.

The girls were well trained and very good at their jobs. The first thing they'd do when they returned from walkabout was to carry over buckets full of goat manure from the goat yard to dig into the old garden beds. When this was done they'd ask me for the seeds and I'd start them off in small beds which they nursed very carefully, especially if there were any late rains. As soon as the seedlings were ready to plant out they'd call me to inspect the beds they'd prepared. If I approved they'd begin to plant out the seedlings, a little of each variety into one end of each bed. From then on they'd continue planting out a few rows every week until the beds were full. This ensured that we had a regular supply of the various vegetables right through the dry season. They certainly knew what to do better than I did that first year, but they were very careful of Kajirri's ego and always made sure I approved of anything they did.

I taught the girls to plant the potato eyes from the peelings and any rotten ones that came in the few bags of fresh potatoes we received each year, and I told them to watch out for termites, as these pests loved both the ordinary potato, as well as yams. From then on they inspected each patch every morning until eventually they came running to tell me, 'That one cheeky bugger ant 'im bin come up now, Kajirri.' I told them to dig the whole patch up at once. They were only small potatoes, but oh, how much everyone enjoyed them, they were so sweet!

Once the garden started producing, every morning after breakfast I'd go down to collect the vegetables I'd need for the day, and give the Aboriginal girl who was cooking for the Aboriginals her share. I also had to check the ripening paw paws and tell the girls which ones to pick. There were three girls in the garden and on top of the watering I'd set them a few other tasks for the day. The water for the garden came from a horse trough up by the windmill. When the girls were ready to water they'd place a heavy stone on the float in the trough which would cause it to overflow, and the water would run down a channel into a pit in the garden. From there they'd water the garden by hand with buckets. On windy days the natural overflow would also run down the channel, and any surplus would carry on down to the creek. I was very proud of the Mt. Sanford garden, but I admit that I did very little of the actual toil in it myself. The girls did most of the hard work and for their efforts I always made sure they had their fair share of what was produced.

I'd only been at Mt. Sanford for a few weeks when I awoke one night to hear the most peculiar sounds. One was a long drawn out mournful call and the other was deep and sad. I listened for a while. They seemed so eerie in the still of the night that I was glad George was sleeping peacefully beside me. Then I remembered someone saying that curlews and mopokes often called in the still of the night and realised I must be hearing these two birds. I crept out of bed and stole to the back veranda and looked out. Just for an instant in the moonlight I saw a long-legged grey bird run behind the kitchen. I knew this must be a curlew because I knew that mopokes were owls. I think the curlews were attracted to the Aboriginals' kitchen fireplace because bits of fat and meat were often dropped there. All became quiet again, so I went back to bed.

Over the years I often woke up and listened to these birds, but I never got used to their lonely, mournful cries. There is no more sad and lonely sound to be heard in the bush at night and it's no wonder bushmen talk about them. George was often away with the stock camp for six to eight weeks at a time and I disliked the quiet moonlit nights when the birds' calls woke me up and I was alone in the house. I had to remind myself that the girls were down in the camp not far away and would hear me if I called out.

I soon discovered that there were plenty of snakes around Mt. Sanford and I always kept a wary eye out for them. Once I found one in our dressing room, but luckily the men were home at the time and George killed it. Another time George was attacked by a large taipan on the back veranda. It was behind a locked box which held the supplies of tobacco for both Aboriginals and whites. When George went to get some tobacco the snake suddenly came out from behind the box and attacked him. He turned and ran, and then came back with a length of fencing wire and killed it.

I had a run in with a snake one time when I was home by myself. I'd woken from my afternoon nap feeling rather groggy from the humidity, so I decided to have a quick shower before going over to re-kindle the kitchen fire. As I stepped off the back veranda a huge black snake made off. I screamed out to the girls and looked around for a weapon, but couldn't see anything suitable, all the while keeping an eye on the snake. Little Topsy who was only about five feet tall came careering through the gate. She took one look at the snake and grabbed the nearest prop from the clothesline, a sapling about nine feet long and quite heavy. She hefted the pole like a highlander preparing to toss the caber, and then brought it down with a whack – at least three feet behind the snake! Then she gave chase around the yard, but the pole was so heavy it always came down way behind the snake. Soon the other girls arrived and when they saw how Topsy was going they all broke into uncontrollable laughter. Of course, once they began to laugh I couldn't help but see the funny side of her efforts too.

I'll never forget the look of intense concentration on Topsy's face as she chased that snake around and around the yard. She paused once to catch her breath, then with renewed determination once again took up the attack. After a couple more attempts she finally hit it and broke its back. Then she dropped the pole and I've never seen such a smile of pure joy on anyone's face. She clapped her hands and gave a little jig, and I went up to her and gave her a big hug. Within minutes the girls had raked over the coals in their fireplace and on went the snake – there was no need for me to get them any afternoon smoko that day! Later as I drank my cuppa on the front veranda, one of the girls presented me with a piece of well-done snake. It looked just like chicken, with very white meat, and it tasted good, too.

Talking of snakes reminds me of an incident that happened on a cold dry season night. As usual I went to bed before George and when my feet got to the bottom of the bed they suddenly struck a cold object. I shot out of bed, badly shaken, thinking a snake had got in to get warm. I quickly called George who grabbed a stick and carefully began to peel the bedclothes back. The tension mounted as he slowly moved the bedclothes back further and further. I stood well behind my brave husband, peering fearfully out. The next thing George gave a horrified yell and jumped back, nearly knocking me over, and he rushed past me with the words, 'Oh! It's a bloody frog.' I looked, and there it sat in the middle of the bed, a great big green frog. I picked it up and took it out to the banana patch, and could hardly walk for laughing. George loved snakes and would catch and play with them for hours, but he loathed frogs and always called me to get them out of the bathroom whenever one moved in.

Women's Business

A few weeks after mum left, George was sitting on the veranda sewing some blinds to keep out the rains, which were expected very soon. I was teasing him about something and he suddenly jumped up and began to chase me. I don't know how it happened, but I tripped and fell full length on the concrete, and knocked the wind out of myself. The next day I had a large bruise on my stomach and didn't feel very well. I curled up on the bed with a hot water bottle to ease the pain. After about ten days I became really concerned that something was wrong as I had been menstruating all this time. The nearest radio to call the Flying Doctor base was at Wave Hill station, so George and I set off on horseback, with a boy to manage the packhorses and spares.

I don't remember much about the trip except that it rained nearly all the way and we camped one night beside a billabong where all the frogs were in full chorus. Some would sing out 'ribbit', 'ribbit', and others 'quart pot', 'quart pot', and big bullfrogs would chime in with 'two bob', 'two bob'. We arrived at Wave Hill and learned from the doctor at the Wyndham radio base that I'd had a miscarriage. I was stunned, as this had never occurred to me. We stayed the night there and then moved back to the police station, about eight miles closer to home. We stayed there for a couple of days, playing cards at night with Slim Edwards and his wife, before returning home. No wonder I'd been so sick on the plane to Timber Creek – I'd fallen pregnant on my honeymoon.

We'd been married in September and George had promised the Magnussens we'd spend our first Christmas with them at VRD. We'd have to ride the sixty-odd miles as Christmas time was the wet season and the roads were closed to vehicles. It meant crossing dozens of creeks and passing through the Wickham Gorge, and it turned out to be quite a trip. We set off in a light drizzle, but by nightfall it was raining solidly. Gibby Creek was running a banker when we reached it, and we were going to have to cross it about thirteen times. We made camp there and the two boys we'd brought along made a lovely soft mattress for my swag from the new growth of sweet-smelling spinifex, but I didn't enjoy it for long. Just after we went to bed the heavens opened and the rain teemed down. The creek rose even higher than it already was and overflowed its banks.

The boys soon woke us as they'd put their tent between our tent and the creek, and had been flooded out. There was great confusion for a time while George and the boys hurriedly gathered the packsaddles and riding gear and piled it in the centre of our tent. I ended up on my swag on top of the pile while the men perched where they could. At one stage water began trickling into the tent so the men hastily dug a trench around the outside to divert the flood. The smell of wet, horsey leather, saddle blankets and four unwashed bodies in a tightly closed small tent! I don't think I managed a deep breath all night. To top it off, the musky scent of the boys was overpowering. I believe we smell just as bad to them so I guess the two boys didn't enjoy that night any more than George and I did. When daylight dawned, four very damp, weary people began to sort themselves out.

It was a beautiful morning and you can't imagine the relief it was to poke my nose outside the tent into the crisp clean dawn air. The sun came up with a big grin of cloud across its face, as much as to say the previous night had been a big joke. George sorted out the gear while I got a hasty breakfast ready. The boys soon mustered up the hoppled horses and in no time we were saddled up and on our way. The creek had gone down since the rain overnight and the water was only up to the horses' knees as we splashed across, but when we reached the Wickham Gorge we found the river in full flood. The track followed the bed of the river so we had to use an alternative route, a narrow cattle-pad high up the sides of the hills. No one dismounted to walk their horse along the pad, so I put on a brave front and rode too, but believe you me, it was so narrow and the hills so steep that I was longing to get off and walk.

We were about halfway through this stretch when for some reason the boy in the rear shouted at the spare horses, urging them on. There was no room for them to pass one another, but some of them tried anyway. They went uphill of the track and came very close to me. These were all spare riding horses, but one packhorse, Maryanne, tried to do the same and pass her mate in front. As she tried to go up the steep slope of the hill the weight of her packs made her over-balance and she tumbled backwards, end over end down the hill, and landed in a quiet backwater of the river. Luckily for her the girths broke and she lost the packs and saddle which enabled her to swim ashore. The boys soon caught her and when George examined her he found that she'd staked herself on a sharp stick. We had to leave her, but she turned up back at the station a few months later none the worse for her ordeal, and I was very pleased that she'd survived as I liked Maryanne. She was a quiet gentle brown mare and I often thought she was wasted as a packhorse.

The men spent the next couple of hours diving for the lost gear and catching another horse to carry the packs, and then we continued on through the gorge. I'll never forget how terrified I felt when Maryanne came crashing down the hillside, almost on top of me – I was petrified! – and I must admit I walked the rest of the way, leading my horse. It was not very far before we came down from the hillside into a little open glade of river gums surrounded by the hills. There we disturbed a pack of dingoes worrying a small mob of cows and newborn calves. They were trying to cut out a calf from the herd, but both dingoes and cattle ran off at the sight of us. Dingoes were thick in this country and many calves were lost to them each year.

George took the opportunity to check on the brands of a few of the cows – they were all Charlie Schultz's Humbert River brand. He knew that Charlie regularly mustered and branded the area because the Aboriginals always kept him informed of where Humbert River was mustering. Charlie was welcome to any branders he could get in this country because although it was part of the VRD lease it was very rough, and the Mt. Sanford plant had its hands full mustering black soil areas where there were large numbers of cattle. They only made a general sweep once in a while for any bullocks they could find in this rough country. George would've been happy to send a couple of boys over to join Charlie in his musters, just to pick up any VRD bullocks, but Charlie preferred mustering on his own.

We camped the night in the little glade and George showed me how to strip bark off one of the trees and use the soft dry inner-bark to start a fire when everything else was soaked. He placed my wet boots by the fire to dry and I'll never forget the look on his face the next morning when he brought the boots to me. They'd been a beautiful pair of R.M. Williams hunting boots that came nearly to my knees. I'd had them for years and they were very comfortable, but now they were midget sized and quite useless. They'd been left near a log which burnt down during the night until the coals were quite near them. As a result they became too hot which caused the leather to shrink quite dramatically. George and the two boys looked very worried – I guess that they thought I'd be in a temper to have my beautiful riding boots ruined – but the little boots looked so ridiculous sitting in the hands of my six foot tall husband that I burst out laughing. Soon all of us were roaring with laughter, especially the two boys who thought it a huge joke. Luckily I had a spare pair of walking brogues in my swag, and the rest of the trip to VRD was uneventful.

After the Christmas and New Year celebrations we set off for home. We'd been riding for about two hours when I started to feel unwell. 'Too much partying and late nights', I thought, but by lunchtime I was feeling decidedly queasy. George opened a small tin of cherries, a very precious commodity in those days – in fact they were the first I'd seen as tinned fruit and vegetables only came onto the market after the end of the Second World War. Cherries were a real luxury at the time, but I could only manage a little of the juice. By the time we camped that night a pannikin of tea was all I fancied, and it was the same at breakfast and lunch the next day. Early that afternoon George spotted a wild cow with her calf, and gave chase. When her first mad dash was over he jumped from his horse, grabbed her by the tail, and when her two back feet were off the ground and she was off balance, he gave a quick jerk sideways and threw her to the ground. Then he quickly tied her two back legs

The Victoria River Downs homestead complex from the air, taken some years after Lexie arrived there The building among the trees at the left is the 'Big House' To its left is the old homestead and the long white roof at the top, left is the store

Courtesy Jones Collection

Frank Spencer standing in front of the old VRD homestead

Courtesy Schultz Collection

The store (centre) where Lexie began work on VRD. At the right is the office and on the left is the saddlery

Courtesy Roden Collection

The Martin Brother's trucks unloading in front of the VRD store, c1950

Courtesy Garner Collection

The open air picture 'theatre' at VRD in 1950

Courtesy Cornish Collection

Frank Spencer, Gwen Magnussen and Hartley Magnussen with children in front of the Big House, c1949

Courtesy Bovril Collection

Packhorses waiting to be loaded at a typical stock camp on VRD, 1950

Courtesy Mahood Collection

Frank Spencer, 'the Speckled Hen', riding a mule

Courtesy Roden Collection

VRD buildings from the water tank
Left to right: the office, store shed, school and the house where Lexie and Nat lived
Courtesy Stan May Collection

The 'blacks' camp' at VRD in 1948
Courtesy Cornish Collection

Roley Bowry, the VRD saddler when Lexie first arrived on VRD

Courtesty Schultz Collection

Jack Roden, the VRD bookkeeper when Lexie arrived, and his wife Belle

Courtesty Roden Collection

Lexie and Nat's 'house girl' Nellie at right. The white girl sitting in front is Veronica Roden, the bookkeeper's daughter

Courtesty Roden Collection

A rare view of the inside of the VRD store, taken two years after Lexie worked there

Courtesty Stan May Collection

Frank Spencer nursing Miff Iverach (Alf Martin's grand daughter) under the overseer's and visitor's quarters. Note the rough and improvised furniture, and the loose flagstone floor

Courtesty Martin Family Collection

Ida and family, King Brumby, Mabel and Tiger at VRD, 1948

Courtesy Cornish Collection

On the Wickham River, the dinghy used by Lexie to cross the river to meet the planes

Courtesy Cornish Collection

A Dragon Rapide, one of the planes that Lexie met at VRD
Courtesy Cornish Collection

The Avro Anson, another of the planes that Lexie met
Courtesty Stan May Collection

'Sailor Jack', VRD 1950
Courtesy Cornish Collection

'Tragedy' Wilson at the VRD races, 1950
Courtesty Mahood Collection

A beast at the bronco panel at VRD in 1952
Doug Campbell is holding its head while Charcoal is castrating it
Courtesy Gerry Ash Collection

Doug Campbell giving a horse its first ride, Gordon Creek, VRD, 1950
Courtesy Gerry Ash Collection

Charlie and Hessie Schultz with Betty, Donna and Richard, c1952

Courtesy Cornish Collection

Jasper Gorge in 1953

Courtesy F.H. Johnston collection, National Library of Australia

A gathering for Donna Schultz's fourth birthday.
Left to right at back: Gwen Magnussen, her sister, Hessie Schultz holding Betty, Fay Hawson-Clarke and Peter Cornish.
Centre row: Dorothy Coleman, Donna and Betty's nursemaid.
Front row: Lexie, Donna Schultz, Robin Magnussen, Pam Magnussen and the Cornish children

Courtesty Cornish Collection

The Magnussen family. Hartley plucking a turkey, and Gwen with Robin and Pam

Courtesy Sam Cook Collection

Afternoon tea at VRD.
Left to right: Hartley Magnussen seated on ground, Nat Gurr, Hessie Schultz, unknown, and Lexie, c1949

Courtesy Cornish Collection

VRD school teacher Fay Hawson-Clarke with Robin, Marg, Pam and Barry, 1949

Courtesy Cornish Collection

Bob Barnes, the head stockman at Centre Camp, and Gerry Woods, 1951

Courtesy Mahood Collection

Jenny Absolom, Alex Woods and Pam Magnussen, c1950

Courtesy Cornish Collection

A truck bogged on the main road between Montejinni and VRD, October 1951

Courtesy Cornish Collection

Drafting cattle in Dashwood Yard, VRD

Courtesy Walkabout Collection

Jack Woods and son Alex at the VRD carpenter's shop, c1950

Courtesy Cornish Collection

Stockmen holding cattle on a drafting camp, VRD, c1950

Courtesy Gerry Ash Collection

Pigeon Hole homestead, VRD
Courtesy Roden Collection

Yarding cattle on VRD
Courtesy Roden Collection

Constable John Gordon at Timber Creek, 1950
Courtesty Mettam Collection

Cutting out a bullock on VRD
Courtesy Walkabout Collection

Counting cattle over to drover Wason Byers (left), near Dashwood Yard, VRD
Courtesy Walkabout Collection

Frank Spencer, Hessie Schultz holding the VRD Cup, Hartley Magnussen and Charlie Schultz, VRD races, 1950

Courtesy Cornish Collection

At the VRD races in 1950

Left to right: Mary Chamberlain, George Bates, 'Tragedy' Wilson, Natalie Gurr, Roley Bowry, 'Splinter' Prendergast, Jenny Little and (seated) Peg Tindal

Courtesy Mahood Collection

'Studying the starters' for the 'Blackfellow Race' at VRD 1949
Left to right: Fay Hawson-Clarke, unknown, and Lexie
Courtesy Bovril Collection

Lexie after wining the Ladies Race, VRD 1949
Courtesy Gordon Collection

Lexie Bates, Hessie Schultz, Donna Schultz, Dorothy Wiseman and Charlie Schultz at the VRD races, 1956

Courtesy Sampson Collection

The Humbert River Camp at the 1956 VRD races
Charlie Schultz is pointing to the right

Courtesy Sampson Collection

At Lexie's wedding, bridesmaid Natalie Gurr and flower girl Pam Magnussen
Courtesy Cornish Collection

Lexie on the escarpment above Timber Creek. This was taken when she stayed at Timber Creek for a few days on her way back to VRD after her honeymoon
Courtesy Gordon Collection

Timber Creek police station, 1953
Courtesy Stan May Collection

Lexie on her way back to VRD through Jasper Gorge, after her spell at Timber Creek, 1950
Courtesy Gordon Collection

Mt. Sanford homestead, c1952
Courtesy Gordon Collection

Alex Brown and Alf Absolom at Shoeing Tool bore, VRD, 1950
Courtesy Mettam Collection

Mt. Sanford homestead, 1953

Courtesy Stan May Collection

The garden at Mt. Sanford in 1953

Courtesy Stan May Collection

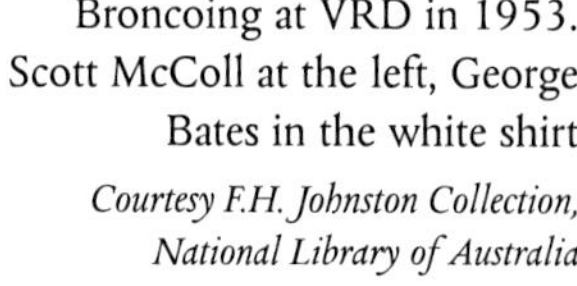

Broncoing at VRD in 1953. Scott McColl at the left, George Bates in the white shirt

Courtesy F.H. Johnston Collection, National Library of Australia

Dragging a wild bull up to a bronco panel at VRD in 1953
George Bates is about to place a leg rope on the animal
Courtesy F.H. Johnston Collection, National Library of Australia

The bread oven at VRD.
Lexie used a similar oven
at Mt. Sanford
Courtesty Walkabout Collection

The Flying Doctor plane with Sister Nichols and Pilot Jack Slade, 1951
Courtesy Cornish Collection

Bill Crowson, the man who drew the Montejinni block when VRD was partly broken up in 1952
Courtesy Mettam Collection

A station truck on the rough track to Mt. Sanford in 1953
Courtesy Stan May Collection

A truck load of Mt. Sanford Aborigines in 1953
The white man and white woman are probably the then Mt. Sanford head stockman, Reg Sammon, and his wife

Courtesy Stan May Collection

Bill Parry, the VRD bookkeeper when Lexie stayed there temporarily in 1953

Courtesy Stan May Collection

Scott McColl amongst wild bulls shot near Waterbag Yard, VRD, 1953

Courtesy F.H. Johnston Collection

Pupils at the VRD school in 1953

Courtesy Stan May Collection

Boundary rider Fred Schull with his donkeys at Mt. Sanford, 1953
Courtesy Stan May Collection

Fred Schull's donkey team
Courtesy Walkabout Collection

Mistake Creek homestead in 1948
Courtesy Walkabout Collection

together with a leather belt. George then proceeded to milk the cow directly into a pannikin and handed the cup to me. The smell of the hot fresh milk made my poor stomach heave so when George released the cow and mounted his horse again I got him to carry it for me until it cooled. Then I managed to slowly sip it down.

That was the last thing I had for a couple of weeks. We arrived back at Mt. Sanford late that afternoon and I went straight to bed and stayed there. I couldn't lift my head from the pillow and for days all I could manage to keep down was a few sips of water. Yes, I was well and truly pregnant! After about a fortnight I still hadn't had anything solid, so late one afternoon George went for a walk up towards the cattle yards with his shotgun. That night I ate two quails for my tea and kept them down – at last I was on the mend. A few days later a boy arrived with the mail. George had been so worried he'd written to Mrs Magnussen for advice on what to do for me, and she sent me a parcel of homemade dry biscuits and the recipe for the cook to make more. She also sent a very green peach, but much to my sorrow it never ripened.

When I was well again I came out of the house one afternoon to find everyone gathered around Alice, one of the garden girls, who had brought her new baby up to be named and registered. Yellow Bob and Alice had four children, including a two year old part-coloured boy called Rex, who Dave Galton proudly claimed as his. The new baby was also obviously part-coloured, and Dave turned to me and asked who I thought the baby looked like. I immediately said Rex, the elder child, which it did. In fact, to me both babies looked very much like their mother. Dave seemed very put out and declared that some white man who'd passed through on the way to Wave Hill must've fathered the child. He then went off to the kitchen in a huff while the men had a quiet laugh amongst themselves. I thought nothing more of the incident until George came in a few days later to say that Dave was leaving. I felt wretched about the whole thing as I hadn't meant to imply that Dave was the father, but the men had been teasing Dave about the baby and he took my remarks to mean that I agreed with the men. He was so proud of young Rex I was sure he would've claimed the new baby too, if it really was his.

I was sorry to see Dave go because he was a good cook and gardener, and all the girls worked happily with him. His only failure was that he was a hopeless alcoholic and I'd been warned never to have any methylated spirits on the place. There was never any lemon essence in the store, and Dave would stealthily process tins of boot polish to extract the spirits from them. My only argument with him was over my discovery that during our absence over Christmas he'd picked the lock on the sideboard where I had my crystal glasses, and a small bottle of brandy for emergencies. I soon discovered the brandy was gone, and also that one of my precious sherry glasses had been smashed. I was furious! The brandy was replaceable, but the glasses had been a wedding present. I'd carried them safely more than 2000 miles across the continent only to have one smashed by a drunk.

Homestead Jobs

When the men mustered around the homestead area they'd bring the cattle to the homestead yards and it was always interesting to watch them brand the calves and the cleanskins – the older beasts which had missed being mustered when they were calves. At Mt. Sanford that first year, by the time branding came around I was five months pregnant and becoming a bit ungainly. I'd only been forty-four kilos when I got married, but when I got sick my family had a doctor friend prescribe a tonic for me. This I dutifully took and my appetite improved enormously, so much so that I put on a lot of weight.

One morning one of the girls and I took the morning smoko up to the men who were branding cattle at a bronco panel. A bronco panel is a fence about four feet high with a vertical slot in the middle and the top rails on both sides of the slot sloping down to the outer ends. Animals to be branded are lassoed by a man riding a bronco horse, usually a semi-draft horse, and dragged up to the bronco panel. A greenhide bronco rope was used, and it was attached to a special harness of breastplate and surcingles which meant that the horse did all the pulling on its chest. The catcher rode into the mob, slowly twirling his greenhide rope over his head until he saw an unbranded beast. He'd cast the noose over the animal's head and the horse would immediately take up the slack and pull it up to the panel. As it passed around the end of the panel, the rope rode up the sloping rail and dropped into the slot. Even large bulls were caught in this way, although sometimes the horses had to really dig in their toes and pull and strain to get them up to the panel.

As soon as the beast came close to the panel, two men with fore and aft leg ropes moved in and catch them. A sharp pull on these ropes made the animal fall over. The head rope was then released and the horse and rider would go back for another, and meanwhile the calf would be castrated, branded, earmarked and released to run back to the mob. Any bulls had their horns cut off. Blood would spurt from the horn stumps for a short while and the small loss of blood helped to quieten the animal down. Cows sometimes came in with their horns growing curled into their head, and George always saw that these were attended to. Some were not a pretty sight and would have died when the horns grew into the brain.

It always amused me to see the white men and the Aboriginals collecting the testicles as the cattle were castrated. After the branding was completed the coals of the branding fire would be covered with cooked testicles. Some of the men thought they might acquire some of the strength of a bull if they ate them. I was told they taste like sweetbreads, but I didn't fancy trying them myself.

This particular year George was short-handed so soon as the men finished the smoko he got me working on the bronco panel. My job was to stand behind the panel and as soon as the head rope fell into the slot, pass a rope over it and hold it down. This was to stop the bulls from raising their heads high enough to jump the panel while the boys were trying to put leg ropes on it. The thing that worried me was, what if a bull jumped the panel before I could get the rope anchored? Can you imagine how I felt? I was just a few feet from an enormous, enraged bull, madly tossing its huge horns and glaring at me between the rails of the panel, its hot breath blowing into my face. Little did the bull know that it only had to surge forward and jump over the rails to be on top of me, but I knew! Needless to say, from then on when they were branding bulls I avoided the branding yards. I was getting far too slow and unwieldy. I went from just under forty-four kilos to ninety-seven kilos with that first baby, and I often wondered what would have happened if I'd missed with my rope and a bull had jumped over to my side of the panel.

Bronco horses could be used for other jobs, too. The old saddle shed at Sanford was very small and dilapidated, so George decided to build a new one. He spent several days sharpening axes on the grindstone in the back yard, and then sent the horse-tailer out to bring in the two bronco horses. When the horses arrived he took everyone out to the nearest stand of sizeable trees and soon had them felling and trimming logs. Each horse was harnessed with a set of chains, instead of the usual greenhide bronco rope, and they dragged each log back to the station. This took a few weeks to accomplish as the horses could only make two trips a day, and when he had sufficient for the new shed he sent most of the people off on walkabout. Then the position of the posts was marked and two boys George had kept back from walkabout were set to work to dig the postholes.

Meanwhile the posts were dressed and squared off. There were two adzes and I was soon nearly as proficient as George at using one. I quite enjoyed this as a change from cooking all the time, although I didn't get out of that job. However, with just our family and a skeleton staff, and with no early breakfasts to get ready, I could spare an hour or so a day. Soon George had all the posts cut to the right length and the ends made ready to take the beams. It seemed no time at all before all the uprights were in and the crossbeams bolted in place. George had ordered sheets of corrugated iron for the roof and sides, and this was soon nailed on. A dividing wall was put in, with one end becoming the new saddle shed and the other end a workshop, and everything was completed before the saddler arrived to repair all the gear for the next season's work.

The greenhide ropes used in broncoing were made on the station. Each time we had a killer the hide was kept and the next morning was scraped clean of any flesh or fat. Holes were cut around the edges of the hide and laces were used to stretch it tightly over an iron tyre from a wagon wheel. Coarse salt was rubbed on the flesh side and it was left to dry. There were two of these iron rims at Mt. Sanford and after each killer a knife was run around the inside of the rim with the driest hide, and the new hide put in its place.

When a new rope was required George would get the boys to soak a hide down in the spring. Then, using a very sharp knife, he'd cut round and round the circular hide until he had one long strip of greenhide of uniform width, and soft and pliable enough to work. When he had three or four strips he'd tie them to a ring attached to a swivel, and fix the swivel to a stout post. The other ends were tied individually to other rings and swivels and these swivels were tied to heavy logs some distance away. A stout stick was thrust through each ring and turned, twisting up the strand. Care was taken that they were all twisted evenly, and when each strand was twisted enough, all the strands were twisted together to form a rope. This was left stretched out tight for days until it dried, and then it was cut from the weights. One end was neatly spliced to ensure that it didn't unravel, and the other end was left attached to the ring.

When it was to be used the rope was passed through the ring end to make a lasso and the other end attached to the bronco gear. All the branding was done with these greenhide ropes and I always loved to watch the boys on the bronco horses moving through the mob. A good man rarely missed his cast for a cleanskin, and immediately the horse felt a beast on the other end of the rope it would turn and drag it up to the bronco panel, with no directions from the rider.

As well as making bronco ropes there were various other jobs that had to be done around the homestead. One was curing the horsehair, used for stuffing the saddles. Before the horses were let go at the end of the season the boys would spend several days pulling their tails. The horses never seemed to mind this as it was done one or two hairs at a time. The girls then gathered this hair strand by strand into small bunches. One girl would hold each end and twist it until it was tight. Then another would hold the twist in the centre while the two ends were brought together and tied. When they let the strands go, they would twist up together. These knots of hair were then placed in a drum of water and boiled, cooled, and spread out to dry. When thoroughly dry they were untied and the hair was nicely curled. The girls then had the tedious task of teasing the hair until it was a curly mass and ready for the saddler to use.

Watching a good saddler at his craft is another story again. Sometimes a saddler wasn't available and George had to do the best he could himself. He didn't make a bad job of this work either, although he never tried to tackle the difficult jobs such as remaking a broken saddle. This he always left to the experts.

Making soap was a chore I had to learn. All the fat was collected from each killer and rendered down by the girls until a bucketful was on hand. It was then put into a copper with a small amount of water and rosin. When it was boiling a small amount of caustic soda was gradually added. This caused the mixture to seethe and boil furiously, and at this critical stage one of the girls always stood by with a tin full of cold water to douse the mixture if it looked like boiling over. Care had to be taken not to add too much water because the excess had to be boiled away before the soap reached the correct consistency. Finally the mixture would be the right texture and the girls would ladle it into specially made tins about three inches deep and three feet square. It was left in these tins for about a week to set and harden a little, and then was turned out and cut into blocks about three inches by four inches. Again, it was left to harden. This soap was issued to all the Aboriginals each week as part of their rations, along with their stick of nicki-nicki. At Mt. Sanford I never rationed the soap, but kept it in the laundry for anyone to use, black or white. I couldn't see the sense of rationing something we had in abundance.

I sometimes wonder if any of these old bush skills are still in use. Getting to the nearest store is easy now that there are planes and helicopters, and good roads. In fact, many of the main roads are now bituminised and there are bridges over many of the creeks and rivers. I would also be surprised if greenhide ropes are made at all these days because most of the branding is now done with a crush, and strong nylon ropes are readily available.

When I was seven months pregnant we decided it was time for me to go down to Adelaide. We knew that Alf Absolom would soon arrive with the bore truck and when he did I went with him to Wave Hill where I had to wait for a few days to catch the plane to Darwin. After an uneventful trip I arrived in Adelaide and went to see the doctor who had prescribed my tonic. He took one look at me and the next thing I was on a salt-free diet. Coming from the station where we ate mostly salted meat I found this very hard to comply with. The pregnancy had interfered with my thyroid and this is why I'd gained so much weight. My daughter Merran was born at the Memorial Hospital in North Adelaide on August 29th 1950.

Improvements and Routines

When I arrived back from Adelaide I was delighted to find a number of improvements at the homestead. One was a new kerosene refrigerator. Several of these had been bought for the head station the previous year and they were a great innovation at the time. It enabled us to keep a small amount of fresh meat for a few days from each killer, usually the rump steak and several pieces of rib roast. How lovely it was to have a meal of fresh meat now and then, between all the salt meat.

Another surprise was to find a wireless installed in the corner of the dining room. It was the old pedal radio from Montejinni. This could be powered by batteries, but we had no way of charging them or getting flat batteries to and from VRD, so for a few years it remained a pedal radio. The aerials went up through the roofing iron and connected with a bank of cross aerials, which enabled us to use several frequencies. It still had the old Montejinni call sign of 8MN, and I often recalled with amusement the time I'd heard Mrs Norton, and reflected on the irony of myself now being the caller. I think the advent of a baby might have had something to do with the arrival of all these luxuries, but whatever the reason was I certainly was grateful.

We soon discovered a problem with the aerial arrangement. The local galah population decided that this delightful group of wires had been erected by some kind humans just for their benefit. They always appeared in the afternoon when I was having my afternoon rest and all of the house girls were down at the creek, so I guess the galahs came to have a look at the homestead while all was nice and quiet. Unfortunately, the weight of their bodies made the wires dance up and down and the wooden spacers hit the iron roof with a loud bang. Their particular delight seemed to be to hang by their beaks and swing around and around the insulated wires. This little caper soon had the insulation stripped off which didn't do any good to our radio reception, and it caused my afternoon sleep to be seriously disturbed.

One afternoon I'd had enough. I marched into the dressing room, got George's double barrelled shotgun from the cupboard and loaded it. I quietly went outside and made my way to a white gum tree which grew alongside the dining room. I was going to give those birds the fright of their lives and get rid of them for good. I carefully took aim and pulled the trigger. There was a loud bang, the galahs flew off in a screaming, raucous mass – and I found myself flat on my back! I lay there and watched two feathers floating quietly down. That was the final insult. This was the first time I'd ever used a shotgun, and by accident I pulled both triggers at once. I was pointing the gun straight up in the air and the force of the recoil had knocked me flat. As far as I was concerned the galahs could have the whole aerial. I swore I wouldn't fire a shotgun again, and I never did.

During the four months I'd been away George had been doing the cooking, but I soon took over again. I'd done a domestic science course at school and still had my cookery book from those days, so I set to work in earnest to cook for George and the men. I had two girls as offsiders in the kitchen so all the drudgery was taken out of the job. I had no cake-mix to beat, no vegetables to prepare, and no washing up to do afterwards, but for a green city girl it was still quite a task to provide five meals a day for several hungry men, and believe me, shearers have nothing on young stockmen!

For morning tea I always served something hot like scones, buns, or pufftaloons. These were just flour and baking powder mixed with water, and dropped in lumps into boiling fat until they were golden, and served with golden syrup. Afternoon tea was usually fruitcake. Occasionally I'd make a sponge and if I had any spare cream it would have a cream filling, but I usually made fresh butter from most of the cream I got from the goats' milk. I also made a tin of brownie every bread day. This was dough mixed with a handful of sugar and dried fruits, and an egg if I had one to spare, and spread with dripping. The closest thing to it is raisin bread.

After I took over the cooking I really missed not having a wooden mixing spoon for my cake making. One day I gave one of the boys a tablespoon for a guide and explained to him that I wanted that size, but a flat spoon made of wood, and he soon produced a very good facsimile which I use to this day. I don't know what kind of wood he used, but it's very dark and very hard, probably ironbark.

With the different recipes I tried there quite often was an ingredient or two that I didn't have. This was very frustrating, so I'd experiment with substitutes. For instance, whenever an egg was called for and the hens had gone on strike I used a tablespoonful of custard powder, and a little extra milk. I continually experimented and any failures I had the girls were only too pleased to take off my hands. I was certainly learning how to be a bush cook.

One day I received word via the radio from VRD that Mrs Magnussen and Pamela wanted to come up to see me for the day as Pamela's birthday treat. I was delighted to have visitors coming and early the day they were to arrive I set the girls to beating duck eggs and sugar for a sponge cake. It was my first attempt and I've never made such a magnificent sponge cake since. I don't know if it was the duck eggs or the long enthusiastic beating by the girls, but each half of that cake was three inches high. I couldn't believe my eyes as I took it out of the oven! I filled it with raspberry jam and a healthy dollop of fresh goat's cream, and I have no idea what else I served for Pam's birthday but on the strength of that cake I think Mrs Magnussen thought I was a terrific cook.

Stores were delivered every six weeks and almost everything came by the case, including all kinds of dried fruit and various jams and golden syrup. As soon as the store came under my control I made sure the Aboriginals had their share of everything. The only thing they didn't get was tinned vegetables and tinned butter, which was mostly used in the stock camp, or tinned fruit because we only got four large tins, two small tins and one huge nine pound tin of prunes every six weeks. The prunes were for seven adults and later four children. Word got around via the bush telegraph that there was plenty of tucker at Mt. Sanford, so we always had a full compliment of Aboriginals in the stock camp and plenty of workers about the house. Years later one of the girls commented to me, 'When you were missus, this place number one for tucker, all about prop'ly fat bugger.' I felt very proud of that compliment.

One time several cases of tinned butter arrived with the rations. This was most unusual because normally we only received six tins. VRD never enquired about these extra tins and we didn't ask any questions. At this time the facilities in the bush were about on a par with the turn of the century and to keep the opened tins from going rancid George decided to make a cooler. He constructed a deep box and filled it with layers of charcoal, alternating with tins of butter. He then proceeded to thoroughly wet the charcoal and I saw to it that the girls did so every day. This way it didn't go rancid before it was all used. I'd seen this method of cooling before but I hadn't realised just how the porous charcoal would allow the cool damp air to circulate. It did a surprisingly good job, but couldn't compete with the old Coolgardie safe. These safes were certainly a Godsend to people in the bush before electric light plants made it possible to run cool rooms and refrigerators.

I also had to cook bread. Years before my time someone built a huge bread oven onto the back of the kitchen. It was made from big river stones set into ant-bed, with a doorway made from pieces of flat iron and a door made from an old steel drum. George taught me the mysteries of bread making and how to make yeast from dried hops. On baking day the 'wood boy', Jimmy Broken-tail, would light a fire in the oven and by the time the bread dough had risen the oven was really hot. George showed me how to test the temperature by holding his hand by the door and counting to ten, but his hands were much tougher than mine and if I had time to gabble from one to ten before my hand got too hot it was it about right.

One morning the oven felt too hot so I threw a dipper-full of cold water into it to cool it down. Whoosh! Out came a cloud of steam and ashes, covering me completely. The girls rushed to me, but I hadn't really been hurt, just my face stinging a little from the steam. Soon the girls were in fits of laughter as they tried to brush the ashes from my hair, which was slightly singed in the front. I must have looked a sight. Later I found my eyelashes were gone and part of my eyebrows singed too. I guess I was lucky the steam didn't badly burn my face. Needless to say, if I thought the oven was too hot I never tried that trick again.

Bread making was a chore I could well have done without. When the stock camp was home I had to make it every three days. I used two fifty-pound bags of flour and mixed the dough in a half a forty-four gallon drum, and set the bread about 10 o'clock at night, just before we went to bed. If it was cold weather I set the dough close to the kitchen stove for warmth, and covered it with a piece of canvas and a blanket. If it was hot I left it on the kitchen table where it was cooler. If the men were mustering they had to be gone before daylight to catch the cattle while they were still feeding out on the flats, so I had to get up at 4 am to punch the dough down and work it again before getting the men's breakfast ready.

After breakfast the bread dough would have risen and be ready to work again. Usually Bessie would help me and we'd fill sixteen tins which each held two loaves – thirty-two loaves in all. After another hour the bread would have risen once more and Jimmy would have the oven hot. I'd get the girls to rake out the coals and I'd test the oven. I used a long-handled, flat wooden paddle to load the bread into the oven and a T-shaped iron hook to pull the tins out again. I was a bit clumsy at first, but soon got the hang of it. After the bread was cooked I usually made a rich fruitcake. These seemed to bake much better in the bread oven after the bread was done.

During the wet season I had two big problems making bread. The first was that late in the dry season we were given enough flour to last six months until the truck was able to make a delivery again after the wet, and for the last few months the flour would be full of weevils, grubs, cobwebs and moths. This affected the quality of the flour and it became difficult to get the dough to rise properly. When it got like this I'd get the girls to sieve the flour and spread it out onto a sheet placed over an old iron bedstead. The bed was left out in the sun for a couple of days and this helped to get rid of some of the 'wildlife', and also seemed to put a bit of life back into the flour. It would usually take two bags of un-sieved flour to make one clean bag. When we had heavy rain and I couldn't put the flour out and everyone had to make do with damper instead. Despite all my efforts I could never remove the smell of the weevils and I'm afraid my bread consumption became almost non-existent at this time of the year, although no one else seemed to mind. Maybe I was just too fussy?

The other problem was the yeast. I tried several methods to get it to work properly, adding rice water, potato water and even some of the wheat which I had to feed the fowls. All of these experiments worked to some degree, but none worked well. In hot weather I had to keep the yeast in the water tray on top of the Coolgardie cooler to keep it cool, and in cold weather I had to leave it by the stove at night to keep it warm. Cantankerous stuff, both bread and yeast, and it certainly made me cantankerous at times, too. Those days are long gone, I'm glad to say. Most stations now have light aircraft or helicopters to run into the nearest town and get fresh supplies of bread and perishables.

Until I went down to Adelaide to have Merran all we had was a hurricane lamp and several carbide lamps. The hurricane lamp was used by the cook in the early mornings when he was cooking the breakfast and knocking back the bread. The carbide lamps were fuelled by carbide, a chemical which produces acetylene gas when mixed with water. They were made of strong metal and the top half held water that dripped down into the bottom half which contained the carbide. In the top there was a screw that was turned to regulate the flow, which had to be just right to obtain the best light. The girls collected these lamps every afternoon, emptied out the used carbide and refilled them. After filling the water tank, the screw was closed down tight and then the two halves were screwed together. To light one of these lamps the water screw was loosened to let water drip down onto the carbide, and the gas produced issued out of a small hole on the side. If too much water was released more gas was created than could safely escape, and the lamp would explode. I was always afraid this would happen to me and they became my pet hate.

One evening I went around to the front veranda where George had been sitting reading to find flames curling up from the middle of the lamp he'd been using. I grabbed it, ran out into the yard and threw it as far as I could. The men heard the clatter and came out to investigate, and after a bit of discussion George smothered it with a blanket and peace reigned once again. The girl who had filled it that afternoon had not screwed the two parts together correctly, and had cross-threaded them. This allowed the gas to escape and catch alight. It was enough for me. I never used one on my own again. I couldn't see very well with the hurricane lamp, but to me it was preferable to the carbide, and when I went to bed, George would take it back to the kitchen for Dave to use in the morning.

When I came back from Adelaide I brought a Tilley lamp with me, the latest lighting invention on the market. It made an enormous difference and I was thrilled with it. For a base it had a tank with a small hand pump which held kerosene. Extending from the top of the tank was a thin pipe which curled over at the top, and a specially treated, small silky bag was attached to it. This upper section was enclosed in a glass chimney to protect the bag, which was very delicate. A couple of pumps were made to force the kerosene up, then a match was held to the little bag which quickly became incandescent. With careful adjustment a very good light was produced and I could sit and read my books without straining my eyes. I also bought two small kerosene lamps which could be lit quickly if I needed to get up during the night for the baby. I still have one of these, but what became of the Tilley lamp I'll never know.

A surprise waiting for me when I returned to Mt. Sanford was that my laundry girl, Long May, had also had a baby daughter. She was such a scrawny little thing that I doubted she'd survive, but from the time I started Merran on solid food I always made double quantities of everything and gave half to May's baby. She never seemed to grow any stronger – her little arms and legs were like sticks and she appeared to be double jointed in all her limbs. May told me her eldest son, Bruce, did not walk until he was about eight years old, and he also had the disjointed look, but her second child, Bill (Rahbi was his Aboriginal name), was normal and very robust. I later discovered from Dave Galton that while May was pregnant with this child he'd given her goats' milk every day, but for some reason he hadn't done this during her other pregnancies.

A day came when May brought her baby up to the house for me to name. I asked her what name she liked and she said Sally, so I duly declared that was her name. Normally no one bothered to ask Aboriginal parents what they wanted to call their babies and often would christen them with derogatory names. One I remember was 'Bugalugs'. When he came up to me one day I asked him his name, and I can still see the poor fellows' hangdog look as he answered me. It was obvious that he expected me to laugh, as no doubt most people did. Some years later, May and Sally were sent to the Darwin Hospital to see if anything could be done to improve Sally's condition. When she returned, May, very shame-faced, said that they'd changed her daughter's name in Darwin. It was now Daphne Dogweed. I was furious and never called her anything but Sally, much to May's obvious relief.

One afternoon when I came out of the house to get the afternoon smoko ready I found May and the rest of the girls waiting for me at the back door. I wondered what the matter was as this had never happened before. Everyone had broad smiles on their faces and there was a lot of giggling going on. What ever did they want? May came up to me and patted me on the arm. 'Missus', she said, 'You all about little bit mummy belongin' to my kids. Now I make 'im you sister belongin' to me' – she was adopting me as her sister! She explained that I had helped to 'grow up' Sally, so I was little bit her mother, and May was claiming to be a 'little bit mother' of my children. She gave me the skin name Nowalla. I was so flabbergasted that I forgot to ask what my name meant in her language. I knew that Nowa was water so I surmised it something to do with water. Little Topsy was so excited that she was jigging up and down with delight. I felt like joining her, but for the sake of my dignity I refrained. May then gave me a big hug as did all the girls and we all had a drink of tea and some cake to celebrate. I was now accepted and I was soon to see the benefit of this adoption. Years later I met Sally and discovered that she'd learnt to walk at the age of about ten, but her legs were badly bent and stick-like. She was then married and had three children who were all normal, thank goodness.

Mustering & Horses

When the men were working around the homestead area they got fresh horses from the horse paddock whenever they needed them. Sally's father, Galloping Peter, was the main horse-tailer. Often as I worked in the kitchen at piccaninny daylight I'd hear him bringing the horse plant up to the yards, ready for the day's work. The mob would go galloping past the house with a roar of pounding hooves, and Peter urging them on with a whip – it was easy to see where he got his name! Presently I'd hear him enter the house yard. He'd wait under the beef house and I'd make a billy of tea and call out to him to come and get his early morning 'cuppa'.

One of the most enjoyable events of the year for me was the annual horse muster which took place shortly after Christmas. This was when all the horses in the horse paddock were mustered and brought to the station yards where they were drafted into different lots to be sent to the other mustering camps. Then those that were being kept by Mt. Sanford were broken in. The first year we were on Sanford Frank Spencer brought his horse-tailer and string of horses, and Gerry Woods brought his string of horses up from Gordon Creek, along with two boys who were not on walkabout. With our Mt. Sanford contingent there were ample riders to muster the large stallion paddock.

In the morning I'd get up early to have breakfast on the table by 4 am. A little after four I'd hear the three horse-tailers bringing in the working horses and would put out a billycan of tea for them. By five the men would all be away and peace would reign for a short while until the girls and piccaninnies arrived from the camp for their breakfast, and the daily life of the station resumed. A couple of hours later there would be a thunder of hooves and the cracking of stockwhips as the mob of horses would go by on the way to the stockyards. Then I'd call a couple of the girls to help me take early smoko up to the men.

After smoko the real fun would begin. The three bosses sat on the top rails of the drafting yard and as each horse came through they would decide its fate. The working horses were sent into one holding yard, and the 'breakers' – young colts and fillies old enough to be broken in – into another. This job was finished by lunchtime and the working horses were returned to their paddock. After lunch the breakers were re-processed and the men studied each horse carefully as it came through the yard. George knew them all and could usually tell the dam of each. Some would be considered a bit young and would be put aside for another year. George usually got about a dozen of his own choice and the rest were taken back to Centre Camp. Later a similar number of breakers were delivered to each outstation for them to break in.

The only other time the stallion paddock was mustered was when the new foals needed branding and the young colts had to be castrated. George usually fitted this in after the cow and calf muster and before the Aboriginals left on walkabout. I always felt sorry for the young colts. George took particular care with the special emasculator used on the horses and kept them in a solution of Condy's Crystals to ensure they were clean. Horses are liable to bleed to death from this operation, unlike cattle where no particular care had to be taken.

When Merran was about six months old George asked me if I'd like to help muster the horse paddock. I hadn't been on a horse since the previous Christmas when I'd discovered I was pregnant and had to ride to VRD. I quickly filled a bottle with water and another with goat's milk, and placed these in the refrigerator, and explained to Topsy just what she was to do if I was late in returning. She was to give the baby as much water as she wanted but the milk was only there if I wasn't back by the time the baby wanted her lunch. Topsy sat down beside the pram and gave a smug look at the other girls who were all crowded around. The missus going for a ride and leaving the baby behind was a major event in their lives. 'Me boss belonga bebby', Topsy declared. I knew she'd take great care of Merran and I shouldn't be more than an hour, but I didn't really want to leave her. I knew she'd be thoroughly spoilt while I was away. Certainly no work would be done because they'd all be too busy playing with the baby, and even the garden girls would leave their work and come up to join in the fun.

I put on my riding gear and went out to where the whole stock camp was waiting at the horse paddock gate. George gave me a lovely bay mare with a beautiful long sweeping tail to ride. Her name, appropriately, was 'Broom'. She was quite a large mare so George gave me a leg-up, but he was a bit enthusiastic and I nearly went over the other side and missed the offside stirrup. I suddenly felt very giddy and the landscape seemed to turn over before my eyes. The mare must have sensed my disorientation and moved off quickly with me clinging to the saddle.

The dizziness passed and I settled into the saddle and looked up to see nine pairs of eyes fixed on me in amazement. They all knew I could ride very well so what was the matter with me? For a moment I thought George was going to make me stay behind. I gave myself a mental shake and told them I was ready. Soon we were through the gate and on our way, but what had come over me? I wondered if it was it a reaction to my late pregnancy. I spent a very pleasant morning mustering with the men, but was very stiff and tired by the time I got back home. I went straight to check on the baby and found her fast asleep with the faithful Topsy sitting beside her, singing a corroboree. Later I discovered that I was allergic to heights, a thing that had never troubled me in my life before. In fact, I still suffer from vertigo in a mild form to this day. Even to climb a small ladder, I know I mustn't look down.

I loved to go up to the round yard with the morning smoko and watch George as he handled the horses. He never seemed to mind how long it took to gain the trust of a young horse, and in a few days they'd walk up to his outstretched hand as soon as the noose settled over their heads. Some he even trained to come to his hand at the snap of his fingers. He trained one of my horses this way and I never had any trouble catching it out of the mob. First he'd stand in the middle of the yard as the animal was run in. He'd talk quietly to it for a while until it steadied down, then with a quick toss of the rope he would have it caught. Then he lunged the horse. He'd allow it to run around for a while, then pull sharply on the rope and force the horse to face him. Eventually it would stand facing him even if he only pulled gently on the rope.

When the animal became accustomed to the rope George slapped it all over with a bag tied to the end of a long pole. When it became used to this the next step was familiarising it to a weight on its back and a girth around its body. Eventually the rope was replaced with a pair of long driving reins run through a set of rings placed on a special surcingle, so the horse would get used to the reins as they were pulled left and right. Finally, the big day would arrive when the horse was to be ridden, and I was always surprised to see how few of them bucked. It only took a short while for the animal to learn to move as desired and to obey the reins or stop on command. Each horse was put through this process every day until George was satisfied.

Each day after being ridden the horses were hoppled out to graze on the airstrip and this was the only part of the whole process I didn't like. It distressed me to see them fighting against having their front feet restricted. They would often stumble or fall over, but it was necessary to accustom them to being hoppled when they were out in the stock camp, and they soon got used to it.

As the boys returned from walkabout they were each given a breaker or two, and it was up to them to finish what George had begun. The work would start at daylight in the cool of the morning, and after a long rest period during the heat of the day it was resumed about four in the afternoon. It continued until sundown when the horses were taken back to the paddocks. Horse breaking was a long hot process for both man and beast in the tropical climate, but one I found fascinating, especially when done by a master at the craft and George certainly was one.

The horse muster was a lot of hard work for everyone, but we all enjoyed the break in our normal routines. Even the evenings were a great change from normal, usually spent playing poker and talking until late. No one had much time for sleep, but nobody minded that. I had my usual nap after lunch, otherwise I think I'd have fallen by the wayside.

Living with the Aborigines

Early each New Year, George would check over all the stock camp gear. The tents were spread out to air, and packs and saddles checked to make sure all their straps and leathers were in good order. Then he'd organise a supply of rations and as soon as the country was dry enough the stock camp was off on the bullock muster. This lasted from eight to ten weeks as they mustered from the homestead, around the run and finished up at Dashwood Crossing for the handover to the drovers. After they'd gone I was left with just the Aborigines for company – the girls and their children, and the old men to old to work in the stock camp – and the camp dogs.

One night after the stock camp had left I woke up with the feeling that something was wrong. The house was bathed in bright moonlight, but the curlews and mopokes were silent. I slipped from my bed and checked the baby in her meat-safe cot. She was fast asleep, but I still felt as though there was someone in the house. I crept quietly around the corner to the front veranda. There was nothing there, but I *still* felt uneasy and moved quietly to the back veranda. As I stepped around the corner a snarling face met me, and I froze! It was an unusually large a camp dog, and my heart leapt up into my mouth.

I quickly stepped back and went into the inner dressing room and grabbed my ·22 rifle 'Betsy'. I loaded it, and crept to the back veranda again, but the dog had disappeared. I went to the gate but could see nothing. A curlew called and I knew that the dog had left the yard. It must have jumped over the back gate which was not very high because it was only there to keep Merran in when she began to crawl and walk. I went back to bed and tucked Betsy under George's pillow. The next morning there were giggles from the two house girls when they made the bed and found the gun. I called everyone up and explained what had happened, and told them that if any dog came into my house I would shoot it. Did they understand? 'Yuway', they agreed, 'missus was right', and they promised to keep the dogs tied up at night. I knew they'd soon forget about the tying up, but they'd been warned and I certainly meant what I said.

One day I realised that the number of teaspoons in the kitchen cutlery box was getting low. I thought this was a little strange, so I ordered more from the VRD store. These duly arrived and were put into use, but it wasn't long before they also began to disappear. I couldn't imagine any use the Aboriginals would have for them, but I still asked the girls what was happening to them. They all rushed to the wooden cutlery box sitting on the bench in the kitchen and proudly held up several teaspoons. I went around counting them and showed that four were missing. The girls were very surprised and there were murmurs among them. No, the missus was not about to get angry. I just wanted to know who was taking them and what for? I asked the girls to keep a lookout for any teaspoons they might find about the place. A few days later I surprised a bowerbird in the dressing room and I instructed Topsy and May to always keep the door closed. I didn't want the birds inside the house as I knew they were very mischievous. Then I thought no more about it.

A couple of weeks later the girls went down to the creek after lunch and as usual I settled down with the baby for an hour's rest. Suddenly I remembered that I'd left a pudding baking in the oven. I raced over to the kitchen to take it out and as I came though the door there was a clatter on the bench, and a bowerbird flew out the open window. I looked to see what it had dropped. Of course, it was a teaspoon. I placed it back in the box and placed the box in the men's dining room, which was gauzed in. I now knew what had been happening to the teaspoons and also to the baby's nappy pins that had been mysteriously disappearing. This I'd blamed on the girls, particularly May, as Sally was about the same age as Merran. I knew that all the girls prized safety pins and I always bought some for them when I got the chance. When they came up from the creek for their afternoon smoko I told them the story of the bowerbird. There were shrieks of delight and much nodding of heads: 'Im one prop'ly cheeky bugger that bird'.

The kitchen girls agreed to leave the cutlery in the dining room from then on and to keep the doors shut, and to keep my dressing room door closed, too. I asked the girls if they knew where the bowerbirds bowers were because I was keen to recover my spoons, and we all agreed to forgo our rest the next afternoon and go and look for the bowerbird's playgrounds. After lunch the next day we set off with billycans of cold tea in hand and Merran in her pram. The girls led the way up the horse paddock to a large patch of conkerberry bushes. There were several bowers there with plenty of old white snail shells and bits of shiny broken glass, but no teaspoons or pins. We had a good feed of conkerberries and I decided to let the cheeky birds keep what they'd stolen this time, but I was determined that they wouldn't get any more.

As we made our way back home we came upon an old rivergum which had fallen over many years before. One of the girls made some remark at which the others all laughed. 'What name you bin laugh? I asked. The girls giggled amongst themselves for a bit and then one of them replied, 'That one 'im Topsy tree.' I was puzzled and asked, 'What name 'im Topsy tree?' The girls murmured amongst themselves, obviously debating just how much they should tell the missus. At last they explained that when Topsy was 'Bingy Bingy' (pregnant), she would lie across the tree and the girls would run back and forth across her stomach. Later she would lose the baby. 'What a primitive method of abortion', I thought, but it wasn't my place to interfere with their customs so didn't comment. Later that night I thought about it. Old Barney and Topsy had one son, young Bilgari, whom Topsy adored. I came to the conclusion that as Topsy's husband was a revered old man of the tribe and she was only half his age, she enjoyed the company of the Europeans. It would probably be taken as an insult to the old man if there was any issue from these unions, as a part-coloured child usually wasn't recognised by a keeper of the law. It was certainly a drastic method for her to take, but I admired her for it as old Barney was a big man over the whole district, not just in his own clan.

Soon the dry storms began once again and every afternoon great clouds of red dust would come rolling in from the northeast. One day I looked at the dust cloud coming and told May that from now on she could just make the beds and tidy up in the mornings, and sweep and dust after the dust storm had finished in the afternoons. Her face lit up and a broad grin split her brown face – her morning's work had just been halved. 'Two fella Narkbarn bin fight too much', she said. 'What's that May?', I asked. She giggled and the kitchen girls gathered around, egging her on. Narkbarn was the Aboriginal name for large frogs, so I knew there was an Aboriginal legend behind her remark. With a little encouragement from the girls and me, she related the following:

At the end of the dry season the waterholes in the sky were dry all except for one. Here sat a big frog, covering what was left of the water. All the little frogs gathered about complaining because they couldn't get any water, but they were too small to challenge Narkbarn. Then a second big frog appeared and demanded that the water be released, and a great fight began which caused clouds of dust to rise and float over the land on the wind. This happened every year. Sometimes it took only a few fights to subdue the greedy frog, other years it took several weeks before he was defeated and the rains were allowed to fall once again. This was the commencement of the wet season.

When the rains began I'd watch them coming every afternoon, and it never ceased to amaze me. The rain seemed to follow down the fence line of the horse paddock as though some unseen being was pouring it out of a bucket. All the rain fell in the paddock, but the unfenced area remained dry. It was uncanny how many times it happened. I wondered if it had something to do with the formation of the hills in the distance. Could it be that they funnelled the wind which blew the clouds to make the rains fall precisely in this pattern? I'll never know.

Illness, Injury and Death among the Aborigines

During 1951 an aerodrome inspector came out to Mt. Sanford to choose a spot for an airstrip. He decided on a small plain on a limestone ridge where only very short natural grasses grew and no maintenance would be required. This plain extended from the creek by the house to the stockyards half a mile away, and for some distance further on. George took his gang of men and felled a number of trees at the far end, and a few weeks later the strip was inspected and passed. The Flying Doctor Service then included us on their regular scheduled surveys and it wasn't long before we had our first visit.

On the morning the first plane was due I was busy preparing the morning tea for the doctors, and every time I turned around another kitchen girl had disappeared. The house and laundry girls were nowhere to be seen either. Soon the only one I could see was Topsy, who was minding Merran. In twos and threes they eventually returned from the creek where they'd all gone for a good wash and clean up – even their hair was washed, and squeaky clean. They then sat in pairs and carefully combed each other's hair. What a to-do! They could hardly contain their excitement and kept asking me if an aeroplane was really coming to sit down at this place. At last the plane could be heard and everyone ran to the fence to watch it land and taxi up to the front gate.

Merran was only about ten months old but even she was caught up in the excitement. She'd never crawled, but with a lot of encouragement from everyone had taken straight to walking, and as soon as she saw the Nursing Sister, Meryl Nickol, she took off as fast as her little legs could go and flung her arms around Meryl's knees. Meryl picked her up and gave her a hug, and told me later that she was astonished, as usually bush children were very shy. I asked Meryl to have a look at Sally and she advised me to supplement her diet with condensed milk.

From this time on, calls were made several times a year to check on the general health of the people, both black and white. One visit was from a group of eye specialists, including Dr. Fred Hollows, who were checking for trachoma. Later another group inspected everyone for Hansens disease (leprosy). Several Aborigines at Mt. Sanford were found to have leprosy and a newly discovered drug was left with us to be dispensed each day to the sufferers.

Before the airstrip went in it was unusual for an Aboriginal to be taken to hospital, but with doctors and specialists now coming to Mt. Sanford fairly regularly they were often evacuated for further treatment. There was one thing that arose from this that for a long time I couldn't understand. When any of the sick Aborigines died in hospital they were buried in the cemeteries at Darwin or Katherine. This caused much consternation among the Aboriginals and they became very afraid of going to hospital. I tried to tell them that it wasn't the fault of the doctors – the people who died had just not seen the doctors soon enough and were too sick for the doctors to make them better. Then I discovered that if anyone in the camp was really ill they'd keep quiet until they either got better or died. Of course, this distressed me, but there was nothing I could do about it.

When someone died at VRD their body was first placed on a small platform and covered with branches of eucalyptus leaves. A smoky fire was kept burning underneath the platform for several weeks and around this the mourners would sit, wailing. The women of the immediate family gashed their bodies with big 'sorry cuts', and if it was a man who'd died his widow would gash her head until the blood flowed. After this mourning period the body was ceremoniously buried, and twelve months later a further ceremony was held and the body exhumed. Any flesh still clinging to the bones was carefully scraped away and the bones were tied up into a bundle with strips of paperbark, taken in sheets from the paperbark tree. The deceased person's belongings were added to the bundle – a man's spears, boomerangs and throwing stick, and a woman's coolamon and digging stick. These bundles were then placed in the fork of a tree. There was an area about half a mile from the camp at VRD where there were dozens of these bundles up in the trees, and at Mt. Sanford I discovered that they were pushed high up into crevices in the rocks along one of the creek beds, well above high water level.

For a supply of eggs and as a change from 'beef, beef, beef', at Mt. Sanford we had a dozen leghorn chickens, a drake and three ducks, and over 270 goats. The goats were looked after by an old pensioner, Judy, whose job it was to collect her lunch from the kitchen straight after breakfast and take the mob out bush for the rest of the day. She had to take them well away from the station because given half a chance they'd strip the vegetable garden, and if it was washing day they'd chew anything on the clothes lines. The kids were left behind at the goat yard and as soon as the herd arrived home each afternoon they were let loose to suckle. The goats were locked up each evening, and Judy and the Aboriginal children caught all the kids and penned them on their own for the night. This ensured that we had plenty of milk in the mornings. Later I got an old milk separator from VRD which hadn't been used for years because the goats there had all gone wild, and I made butter from some of the cream.

On several occasions the goats returned well before Judy who no doubt had gone to sleep after lunch. One afternoon the goats arrived home without Judy and I got ready to give her a scolding, but when I saw her coming along she was obviously limping. The girls went to meet her and brought her to me. She had one foot roughly tied up in some blood-soaked rags so I sat her down and sent the girls for a basin of warm water. When this came I added some Condy's Crystals, the only antiseptic in the medical chest, and then unwound the rags. I couldn't believe my eyes! There was a great gash across her instep, and how she'd hobbled home on that foot I'll never know. I questioned the girls and discovered that Judy had found a 'sugar-bag' tree (wild bee's nest in a hollow tree). After cutting the limb from the tree she'd attempted to split it open, but the axe had glanced off and landed across her foot.

Unfortunately for Judy the radio battery was flat, so I couldn't call the Flying Doctor base at Wyndham. I washed the wound and her foot, then threaded a surgical needle I found in the medical supplies. I prayed that I wouldn't do anything wrong, and after getting two of the girls to press the sides of the wound together I began to stitch. I had nothing to use as an anaesthetic, and though it seemed to take forever Judy never flinched or made a sound. By the time I'd finished and applied a firm bandage I was a nervous wreck. I gave Judy a drink of very sweet tea and some aspirin, and told the girls to bring her back next day so that I could change the dressing. I then ran for the toilet where I was violently sick, and shivering and cold. 'It must be shock', I thought, so I prescribed myself a drink of sweet tea and soon felt better. It's funny, but I've found that whenever there's an emergency I can attend to it without having to think about it, but as soon as it's over I go to pieces. I dressed Judy's foot every day and two weeks later took the stitches out, using a razor blade which I boiled on the stove to sterilise it. Apart from a slight limp Judy completely recovered.

Not long after this episode I was having my afternoon tea on the veranda when there was a commotion in the back yard. I didn't take much notice at first, but as it continued I went out to the back veranda and was met by two of the girls leading Norah, one of the garden girls, towards the house. She sat down on the ground at my feet and I could see blood running from a head wound. I sent one of the girls for a bowl of warm water and hurried to the medicine chest for the Condy's Crystals, and a pair of scissors which were always kept sterilised. Before I could do anything there was a piercing scream from the Aboriginal camp. 'That one Lorna, 'im crazy bugger, Kajirri.' One of the girls said. 'She bin hit Norah alonga head with 'im billycan.'

The screaming was coming closer and I looked up to see Lorna charging from the camp, screaming at the top of her lungs and brandishing a large ironwood nulla-nulla. A few days before I'd tried to lift this nulla-nulla, but it was so heavy I had to rest it on my shoulder before I could get it off the ground, much to the amusement of the girls. I went cold. Lorna was completely demented and well past any reasoning, and she was a big woman, twice my size.

I'd made a rule when I first went to Mt. Sanford – there were to be no fights or arguments within the house yard, and I thought of this now. My authority was about to be challenged and what was I to do? The three girls moved closer to me with looks of apprehension on their faces. I dropped the scissors in the basin and ran into the house, snatched up my little ·22 rifle and ran out, just as Lorna arrived at the back gate. 'You no-more come alonga my yard Lorna', I shouted. 'You come inside I shoot you alonga leg. You no more fight-fight along my yard. You go back alonga your camp, sit down quiet fella, no-more fight-fight alonga Norah.'

The screaming stopped as though a tap had been turned off, and Lorna turned and ran back towards the camp, starting to scream once again when she reached halfway. I breathed a sigh of relief. My gun wasn't loaded and what I would've done if she hadn't stopped I don't know, but the bluff had worked. Thankfully I put the gun aside and returned to Norah. She had a nasty gash on the top of her head, and after cutting the hair clear I cleaned the wound and inserted several stitches. Then we all had a cup of tea to settle our nerves. I asked the girls what the row was about and they told me someone had used Lorna's tea billycan to cook a small piece of salt beef. She'd blamed her sister-in-law, Norah, who was the cook that week. No one ever owned up to the crime so I let it rest. After all, who was likely to confess when Lorna was making such a racket down in the camp? I certainly wouldn't have wanted her after my blood.

Lorna continued to scream and yell late into the night, and off and on for several days. She never came up to the house or worked in the garden again, and the girls took all her meals down to her. I sent messages that everything was now all right, but to no avail. A few weeks later the stock camp returned and I told George what had happened – and received a good dressing down! There was no mention of what I *should* have done. A couple of months later the Wave Hill policeman called on his rounds and I told him what had happened. He looked at me for a minute, then said quietly, 'Next time have one up the spout' (a bullet in the gun ready to fire). 'Oh! No!' I replied, 'I could never do that!' For a while I had nightmares in which huge berserk black women came at me with enormous nulla-nullas, but it was not long before Christmas arrived and most of the Aboriginals went on walkabout. George let Lorna and Norah and their husbands go first and they never returned. I was sorry to lose Norah. She and her husband had spent many years with a drover and she was always most helpful and thoughtful about the place.

I often think of that episode in my life and wonder what else I could have done to save Norah from a beating, or worse. I was also amazed at George's attitude. He never left the homestead without his Luger pistol in its holster on his hip. He'd told me that before we were married he'd had to threaten boys with it several times when they ganged up on him in the stock camp. At that time it was the usual practice for white men to carry firearms with them everywhere in case the Aboriginal stock boys became disgruntled with their work or their white boss. They were also useful to kill any old bulls that were caught in the mustering.

Sometimes some of the myall Aborigines who camped across the river at VRD would come into the Mt. Sanford country and spear cattle, and obviously they were always afraid they'd be caught. George ran into a group of them one day just after they'd speared an old bull, but he didn't get angry. Instead, he finished it off for them. He said he felt very sorry for the lot of them because some of them were lepers, and the police were always trying to round them up to send them to Darwin for treatment. One of the men in the group was Davey, a boy we'd had in the stock camp for some time. He was a leper and had a nasty suppurating wound on his leg that wouldn't heal. His wife was Long May, my house girl who told me the story of the frogs fighting. By the time I knew him, Davey could no longer walk and May had to carry him everywhere on her back. One year he went on walkabout, and never returned.

Getting Meat

Almost all the meat we ate on the station was beef, with an occasional goat or chook for variety, but it was always nice to get something else for a change. One afternoon I went for a swim and took my rifle with me to try and shoot some ducks I'd seen further down the creek. All I found was a raucous white cockatoo which seemed to find it very amusing that I'd missed the ducks. It kept up its 'abuse' of me even as I walked past its tree, and in a fit of annoyance I turned around and shot it. It was a thing I wouldn't normally do as I usually only shot what was edible. 'Well', I thought, 'the girls will enjoy it, even if I don't have my ducks'. I arrived back at the house and handed the dead bird over to the delighted girls who immediately threw it on the coals, but just then Jimmy Brokentail came up and saw the bird.

'Where you bin shoot 'im, Kajirri?', he asked. 'Over by the waterhole Jimmy', I replied. A broad grin creased his old face. He quickly turned away and snatched the bird from the fire, and walked off towards the camp, leaving all the girls with long faces. 'What name Jimmy bin take 'im?' I asked. 'You bin shoot 'im alonga blackfella Sundee ground missus,' said one of the girls. 'We fella no more eat 'im tucker from that place', said another, and they all mournfully returned to preparing another meal of salt beef for themselves. I felt sorry for them. A cockatoo would have been a very welcome change of diet for them, just as I'd been looking forward to a nice plump duck. I made up my mind that from then on if I saw any bush game I'd try and shoot it for them, even if I didn't consider it edible myself.

Months later, just before the wet began, one of the stock boys came racing down to the house. 'Boss, Boss, big fella tucker', he yelled, 'you shoot 'im please Boss?' George grabbed the ·303 rifle and we all went out to see what it was. At the goat yard one of the boys was crouched down. Every now and then he would flap his red shirt for a few seconds, then withdraw it again. We looked up the flat and walking past the stockyards was an emu, feeding towards us along the flat. Emus are very curious birds and will come to investigate anything unusual they see – hence the boy flapping his shirt. We waited and watched as he enticed the bird until it was only about 200 yards from the goat yard, but suddenly it saw him and turned to race off. There was a loud report and over it went in a crumpled heap. I hated to see it killed, but to the Aboriginals it was a very welcome feast. We heard them singing and dancing late into the night, and it was a very quiet, tired group of workers who presented themselves for breakfast the next morning. The work about the station went on in a desultory fashion until lunchtime when the boss took pity on them and gave everyone an extended lunch break. I think they all slept the afternoon away, but the next morning a happy and contented bunch reported back for work.

There were two old pensioner men at Mt. Sanford when I first arrived. I can't recall the name of one, but the other was Old Barney, whose wife was Topsy. He'd been 'car boy' for Alf Martin when Alf was the manager of VRD. Old Barney had leprosy and by the time I knew him he no longer had any fingers or toes. He could still ride a horse and held the reins with his thumbs. When the stock camp was out and we needed meat, these two old men would muster up a killer for me. When I saw them returning I'd walk to a group of small trees about half a mile from the house, climb up into the branches with my little rifle, and wait for them to haze the cattle beneath the tree. I'd choose a killer and wait until I had a clear head shot to make the kill.

I'd had a few lessons at butchering and had become quite adept at it so as soon as the other cattle were taken away I'd take a butcher's knife, cut the beast's jugular vein and bleed it. I'd take hold of the tail, place one foot behind the stomach and push rhythmically until all the blood was pumped out. By this time the girls had chopped small leafy branches from the trees and placed them in a heap on one side of the beast. This was to place the meat on to keep it clean. Two girls would take a front and a hind leg each and pull the beast onto its back. I'd then straighten out the neck and force the head back until it was resting on the horns. Next I'd make an incision behind the front leg and insert a pointed stick two feet long that the girls had prepared. The other end of the stick was placed a small hole in the dirt and the girls would carefully let go of the legs to make sure that our propping up would hold. Then it was my job to open the carcase from the head to the tail, making sure that I didn't pierce the stomach. I'd make a slit in the skin up each leg and then the skinning could commence.

As soon as all the skin was removed from each side I'd lay the carcase down and as I cut out each section of the meat I'd throw it onto the heap of leaves. When this was done we rolled the carcase over and cut the meat from the other side. The girls would take the pieces of meat from the leaves and half fill their sugar bags, and then carry them on their heads down to the beef house. It would take me about three hours to kill, bleed, skin and cut up a beast, with frequent stops for a drink of tea as it was hot, exhausting work. After a rest, I'd have to salt the meat. This was done by scarfing – putting long deep cuts into the meat on the cut side and then rubbing coarse salt into the cuts. The pieces were stacked up on the table in a pile with the cut side up to enable the salt to absorb the meat juices and to penetrate through the meat.

George told me I must always do all the salting myself because if the girls did it the meat would probably go bad. I could never make sense of this, but as Dave Galton had always salted the meat I thought that I'd better do as I was told. The next day the girls turned the pile of salty meat, and the second day they hung the pieces from wire hooks on wires stretched about the beef house to allow the meat to gradually dry out. When completely dry it would last for months, but our beef never got the chance to reach this final stage because there were so many mouths to feed.

Goodness, it was hard work all on my own! The job would take me until 8 or 9 o'clock at night, by which time I was exhausted, and after a hasty shower I'd fall into bed too tired even to eat. On killer nights the girls would always bath and feed the children and put them to bed for me, and if any of them cried during the night I certainly never heard them, I was so tired. I sometimes wondered if some of the girls slept up near the house on killer nights to listen for the children in case they woke up. They were always very protective of me and at times I used to wonder just who was taking care of whom!

In addition to shooting and butchering killers, after one of the old pensioners died I had to go out with old Barney and muster the killers as well. It took three or four hours to find a mob in the bush, and an hour or two to bring it back to the yards. We'd leave about 8 am and bring a mob back by 2 pm. This meant that on killer days I'd be on the go for about twelve hours. I've already mentioned my experience of shooting a killer from a tree with a ·303 while I was pregnant. The next time I was pregnant George left a few bullocks in the home paddock so we didn't have to go far for a killer. I then went back to killing from a tree because it was easier than trying to take them to the yards and back each time. At least the trees were bigger in the bullock paddock, and I made sure I had my own rifle from then on.

Second Pregnancy

With my second pregnancy I didn't have morning sickness. About a month before I was due the Flying Doctor took me to Darwin to await the birth of my baby. Natalie came to Mt. Sanford to care for Merran and the next day the plane arrived for me. First we flew to Argyle station where we stopped for lunch with Margery and Eric Durack. There the doctor lanced a large boil on a child, and then we flew on to Lissadell station where we picked up another patient. We arrived at Darwin airport late that afternoon, and the other patient and I were picked up by ambulance and taken to the old Darwin Hospital near Myilly Point. I was admitted to the maternity ward and given a bed with the head against the delivery room. For the next six weeks (the baby was two weeks late) I heard every baby being delivered. I thought it was rather a peculiar spot to put a mother-to-be, but I was mobile and allowed to go out during the day if I wished, so I'm glad to say that it didn't worry me. If it had been my first baby it might have been a different story.

The old hospital was a sprawling affair with only shutters on the outer walls to keep the rain out. There were no wire screens, so the flies, mosquitoes, moths and other insects were a constant nuisance. Each bed had a mosquito net hanging over it which was tucked tightly in under the mattress every night as soon as we finished our evening meal. One night I was curled up on my side, reading, and I'd forgotten to pull my net down. Suddenly an insect attracted by the bed light flew into my ear and began to buzz, and I nearly went crazy until a sister poured some oil into my ear and drowned it. From then on I was careful to pull my net down before putting my light on.

When the contractions finally began I went looking for the sister who I found in the delivery room, busy sterilising a tray of instruments. There was no autoclave there then and I watched as she poured methylated spirits over the lot and dropped a match into it. She must have been a bit enthusiastic with the metho' as flames shot high in the air with a great whoosh. We both took a hasty step backwards and watched the blue flames do their work. I told her of my condition and Malcolm arrived a few hours later. It was St. Valentine's Day, February 14th 1952.

Malcolm was one of twelve babies all born within a few days of each other, and most of them boys. Being the middle of the wet season it was very hot and humid and there was no such thing as an air-conditioner, only large ceiling fans in every ward which stirred the warm air a little. Within a few days most of the babies were suffering from prickly heat so the sisters covered the little bodies with gentian violet. What a sight some of them looked. I was thankful Malcolm was not among those affected, but I felt sorry for the mothers of those who were painted blue all over. The wards were full and the nurses very busy so I was asked to help out in the nursery while I was a 'lady in waiting'. I weighed the babies and took them to their mothers at feeding time, so I got to know most of them fairly well. I quite enjoyed this as it helped the weeks to pass more quickly.

When Malcolm was a couple of weeks old a kindly couple agreed to look after us both for a further week, just to make sure that all was well before we went home. After all, it would be an expensive exercise to bring us all the way back to Darwin if something went wrong. The husband was the Acting Chief Customs Officer and had the customs house on Myilly point, and I spent a lovely peaceful and enjoyable week there. I was amused one day when the lady of the house thanked me for having such a good baby. Apparently her husband had not wanted children because he believed they made too much noise crying at night. Malcolm hadn't made a peep all the time the husband was at home and apparently this made him change his mind!

At last, after over two months away I arrived home with the new baby, and a baby doll for Merran. From then on, whatever I did for Malcolm, Merran did the same with her doll. She was a very caring little person and always mothered children younger than herself. When I'd brought Merran home from Adelaide the carpenter at VRD had made a meat-safe cot for her and I gave Topsy the job of sitting beside the cot with a bucket of water and a single bed sheet. She'd thoroughly wet the sheet in the bucket, wring it out and then drape it over the cot. Any breeze that blew then made it much cooler for the baby. When I arrived home with Malcolm, Topsy was delighted to get back her old job of nursemaid. She'd sit for hours, singing corroboree songs softly to herself while keeping Malcolm cool. I often wondered if this was the reason he grew up to like playing a guitar and composing and singing his own songs.

PART 3

INTERLUDE – MISTAKE CREEK AND URD

To Mistake Creek

One afternoon a plant of horses came up along the road from head station. We all looked to see who it could be, trying to identify the lone stockman. It was the overseer's boy, Bob, with a letter from Frank Spencer saying he'd had an argument with Magnussen, and was leaving. Everyone was upset to hear this news. Frank had worked on VRD since before the Second World War, and I always thought he intended to stay on VRD until he retired. He'd sent a small mob of horses up to George, including my lovely little mare Moonlight and a little bay filly he'd broken in for me before I was married. There were also several of his favourite horses he didn't want to see mistreated by the new overseer, whoever that might be. Frank knew that George loved horses and they'd be well taken care of by him. He later got a job as horse-master on a station in Western Australia, and he stayed there until he died.

The next time we went out mustering, Moonlight was saddled up for me. As I made towards her George called out to a young teenager, Bruce, to try her out first for the missus. As he swung up into the saddle Moonlight took off up the flat, with Bruce fighting to control her. 'Let her head go', I prayed silently. He managed to pull her around in a wide circle and she arrived back in the mob with a rush. Obviously, Moonlight didn't like men with spurs anymore. Poor Bruce was 'white', or as near as an Aboriginal can get to it. He gave me a sickly grin and as he jumped off I grabbed the rains and mounted before George could say I wasn't to ride her. The boys had seen what the mare did with Bruce and were murmuring amongst themselves, and I could feel everyone's eyes on me. I left the reins loose and sat quietly, straight in the saddle, and began to talk to her and pat her on the neck. Her ears twitched and she tossed her head, and then settled down. I drew a breath of relief. She knew who was on her back and I knew there'd be no more trouble with her, and I spent a most enjoyable morning mustering with the men.

A few months later George spoke to Magnussen on the radio, and then came into the kitchen and told me to pack up everything because were leaving in two weeks time. Of course, I wanted to know why we were leaving and more importantly, where we were going, but George wouldn't tell me anything. When the time came a truck arrived to take us to the head station where I had to leave all my things, as we arrived just in time to catch the plane to Katherine. Then we went by bus to Alice Springs to catch the 'Ghan train to Adelaide.

I'll never forget that train trip. There was no such thing as a platform and everyone climbed aboard from the dirt track alongside. When we were about to board the train Merran picked up a large-headed tack, and before I could stop her it was in her mouth and she'd swallowed it. I was frantic and quickly sent George to buy some big black grapes I'd seen a few minutes before, and as soon as we got on board I began skinning and pitting them and feeding them one by one to Merran. I knew she wasn't used to them and I hoped they'd give her a mild tummy ache, and the tack would pass through her. I also gave her some bread to eat in the hope that it would cushion the point of the tack. I spent a very uneasy night hoping the tack would go down headfirst and not pierce her stomach or intestines, and the next morning I was very relieved to find it in her nappy.

All was well and we arrived in one piece at my sister Gwen's. Like many in the post-war years, she and her husband were building their own home. The spare bedroom wasn't quite finished so George took the children off with him into Adelaide, and Gwen and I spent the afternoon finishing laying the floorboards. By this time Gwen was an expert and soon had me clamping and hammering along with her. We finally finished and settled down for a quiet cuppa before the others returned for tea.

George only stayed for a few days before going up to Tennant Creek where he'd found a job helping a contractor build yards and it wasn't long before he sent me a letter saying to meet him in Tennant Creek because he'd got a job managing Mistake Creek station. When we arrived at Tennant Creek we caught a bus up to Elliott where we were met and taken to Nicholson station for the night. The next day we travelled to Ord River station and thence to Mistake Creek, and this is where we lived for the next twelve months.

Mistake Creek was quite different to Mt. Sanford because the main road from Ord River to Spring Creek ran past the door. This meant that I had an occasional visitor and wasn't as isolated during the dry season as I'd been at Mt. Sanford. At Sanford I might see two white women every six months, if I was lucky. There was also a telephone line connecting us to Ord River station, so as long as the line wasn't down somewhere I could get in touch with them in an emergency. George was soon out bullock mustering and was a bit disappointed with the numbers he was getting, but he soon cheered up when told he had mustered up the biggest mob ever seen from Mistake Creek. Later on his branding figures were also much higher than anyone had managed before, but he didn't like the country and I knew he was wishing himself back at Mt. Sanford where he'd been for many years.

Mistake Creek homestead was an old wood and iron building on the banks of the Negri River. It had very rough flagstone floors and we'd only been there a few months when an elderly Italian was sent to pave them properly. He made a wonderful job of fitting and setting the stones and at last I had beautiful even floors right through the homestead. I only knew the man as Joe as he spoke very little English. I fed him as best I could, but I bet he missed his Italian meals. I'd often go down to the river with the girls and piccaninnies in the late afternoon and try to catch a fish. There were plenty of long toms (fresh water gars) to be seen, but they were impossible to catch on a line as they had such small mouths and I often wished I had a net to catch a few.

In June 1953 my third child, Anne, was born at the Wyndham Hospital, and what a funny little place Wyndham was in those days. I was sent there a month before the baby was due and settled in at the Nine Mile Hotel to await her arrival. I was very comfortable there and became very friendly with the cook, and spent many pleasant hours in her domain drinking cups of tea and watching her prepare the meals. She showed me how she made her renowned dish of 'Barramundi au Grautin'. This was on the menu every Friday night and half the township would come out to enjoy it.

One day there was a great hullaballoo as the publican sent a traveller packing. He was told to get into town as he wouldn't be served at the Nine Mile. Later I heard from the cook that this traveller had killed the publican's pet python, a huge monster that lived under the hotel. The traveller arrived just as the snake came out into the car park and, very heroically he thought, he killed the snake and rushed inside to tell his story, only to be met by the irate publican. The reptile had been kept there for many years to help keep down the rats, and was well known in the district. None of the locals would ever have harmed it, and for a few days other travellers passing through were treated very shortly as the publican grieved for his pet.

I used to go into town every week to see the doctor, and at last he admitted me. Anne's birth was induced as she was ten days over due, the usual thing with me, and after she was born I returned to Mistake Creek to a happy welcome from a delighted Merran and Malcolm. An elderly couple who lived at Spring Creek had looked after them while I was away. In fact, they fed them so well that they were both as fat as little butterballs, and I expect they'd been thoroughly spoilt.

A few weeks later an eye doctor and her party passed through and I mentioned I was a little concerned about a lump that was forming in one breast. The doctor examined it and gave me an injection of penicillin, saying that this would fix it. Fix it! By mid-afternoon I felt very tired and off-colour so I decided to lie down for a while, and there I stayed until 10 am the next morning. I remember waking several times during the night, either shivering with cold or burning up with fever, and with agonising pains in every muscle and joint in my body. I have no idea who fed the children or took care of the baby that night. I certainly didn't feed her. The youngest Aboriginal child at Mistake Creek was about two years old, but was probably still being breast fed, so I presume her mother fed my baby that night, bless her. I phoned Ord River the next morning and caught the doctor and her party just as they were leaving. She told me to never to allow anyone to give me penicillin again as I clearly was allergic to it.

It was at Mistake Creek that I received a terrible fright. George was away mustering and one evening Merran came into the kitchen and told me she'd dropped the baby. I rushed to the verandah where we all slept and found Anne still in her crib. Merran was only two and a half years old so I couldn't be sure whether she really had dropped her or had only tried to pick her up. Anne looked all right, and in any case, there was nothing I could do. She seemed quite okay in the following days and weeks, but after a few months I began to think she was slow in her development. The next time I went to Adelaide I had her examined by a paediatrician. He came to the conclusion that Anne was retarded or had been injured. He said she would only learn very slowly and would need care for the rest of her life. Because we lived in the outback he said we wouldn't be able to provide the care she'd need and he advised me to have her placed in an institution. It was only with great reluctance I did this, and I still miss her to this day.

While we were living at Mt. Sanford the Government resumed a considerable portion of Victoria River Downs which until this time had been the largest cattle station in the world. The resumed land was divided into three blocks which were put up for ballot and later became Montejinni, Camfield and Killarney stations. Bill and Vi Crowson in partnership with Bill Tapp drew Montejinni, Camfield was drawn by Michael Vandeleur, 'Ringer' Edwards and Charlie Campbell, and Killarney was drawn by Eric Izod and Ivor Hall. Killarney was later purchased by Bill Tapp and greatly improved by him and his family.

The owners of VRD had known for several years that they were to lose this country so they had plenty of time to muster their cattle from the resumed area, but they never made a real effort to gather the stock or to build fences and paddocks to hold whatever cattle they mustered. The value of the stock would definitely have been greater then the cost of the improvements, but it wasn't until after they'd finished their own bullock and calf musters in the last mustering season that the Montejinni, Pigeon Hole and Mt. Sanford camps were assigned to do a general muster over the resumed area. This meant that the camps were already tired after a full season's work and the Aboriginals were anxious to be off on their annual walkabout. As a result it was a slap-dash affair of only a few weeks duration. I never heard how many branders or bullocks were mustered, but it was too late in the day to do much good and the general consensus was that it was just a waste of time.

The biggest factor in the failure of this event was that there was no fence between VRD and the resumed area. This meant that except for the bullocks which were put into the VRD bullock paddock, any cattle mustered and taken onto the VRD lease couldn't be held there, and by the end of the wet season they'd all returned to their old stamping grounds. Of course, this mismanagement meant that when the blocks were taken over there were still large numbers of cleanskin cattle on them, and these gave those who drew the blocks a good start as far as stock was concerned.

Back to VRD

Just as the build-up began and the weather began to get sticky, George told me Magnussen had left VRD and the new manager, Scott McColl, had offered him a job back on VRD. George went off to Ord River to catch a plane to VRD and arrived back a week later with an old station truck, so off we went once again. We were a bit crowded, with Merran and Malcolm sitting between us and Anne on my lap, but all went well until we pulled up for lunch. When we were ready to move on the engine refused to start. The solenoid was wearing out and the motor couldn't be started while the engine was still hot. Because of this we spent twice as long on that trip through Timber Creek to VRD as we should have, but eventually we arrived safe and sound. At VRD I finally learnt why we'd left VRD in the first place. Magnussen had been sacked, but he must have known this was coming and before he left he got rid of all the best men on the place, hence his quarrels with George and with Frank Spencer. I often wondered if Magnussen's mismanagement of the VRD resumptions might have been one of the factors in his dismissal.

Since I'd married and left the head station, several more houses had been built, arranged in a large horseshoe shape. Looking from my back fence, the furthest on my left was the Absolom house. Next to them lived the family of an Italian blacksmith whose side fence connected with the back of the schoolhouse. Then in a straight line facing the Big House was the single girls' cottage, the bookkeeper's house and our house. Adjoining us on the right, the first was the house of Peter Cornish, the mechanic, then there was the home of Cammy Cleary, the Centre Camp head stockman. Inside the horseshoe was the new kitchen and men's quarters. Here Joe the Italian cook reigned. He made the bread for everyone and I was glad not to have this chore any longer, but once a week I'd make a large batch of fruit buns and send most of them over to Joe for the men's smoko. He was most appreciative. After being so long at Mt. Sanford and Mistake Creek it felt a little strange to be once again living with neighbours around me. It seemed as though I was living in a small village, which I suppose it was.

We were given the old mechanic's house, the third house in the married quarter's row, and we soon settled in, but unlike Mistake Creek where everything had been supplied, we now had to provide our own household goods. George went off to see where the belongings were that we'd had to leave behind when we caught the plane for Katherine the year before. There was nothing in the sheds and we were told that Magnussen had ordered my boxes to be taken to Newcastle Waters and left there. George borrowed the station truck once again and retrieved them, and what a state they were in! All my books had been damaged by water and how I cried over my old friends. My mother had belonged to the Readers Union Book Club, and every three months she'd forward on the latest selection. I also had a standing order with John Martins in Adelaide to send me both the Australian and the English Women' Weeklies, as well as the Georgette Heyer historical novels as each one was published. They'd been my lifeline to civilisation when I'd been alone at Mt. Sanford. I still have most of these books in my library, but of course, some have been borrowed over the years and never returned.

Thankfully my linen was all right because it had been packed in my steel cabin trunk, along with all my glassware and china. My poor Singer treadle sewing machine was a little rusted, but the mechanic kindly cleaned it for me and got it working again in no time. The boxes had been just left on the side of the road at Newcastle Waters and they sat there until it began to rain. Then the owner of the hotel had them carried onto the side veranda to await the arrival of the owners, God bless her. What a contrast her kindness was to Magnussen's pettiness.

One of our neighbours was the new bookkeeper, Bill Parry, and his wife Honour. They had two little girls who were a few years older than my children, but they were all soon playing happily together. It was there one night that I was woken up by a little voice calling 'mummy'. I was out of bed in an instant and with a torch went to check that everything was all right. I wasn't really sure whether I'd heard anything or had just been dreaming. Merran was fast asleep and so was Malcolm. Then I took a second look at Malcolm because his face seemed to be flushed. I put a hand on his forehead, and he was burning hot. I placed the thermometer under his arm and took his temperature, and it showed 108.6 degrees. I nearly dropped the torch with shock! What was it I had to do? Sponge him in cold water? Or was it warm water? I was in such a state I couldn't think. Then I remembered that Honour next door was a nurse. I flew outside and scrambled through the dividing wire fence. 'Honour are you awake?' I called. Bill's sleepy voice answered and I told him that Malcolm was very sick. He woke Honour and she followed me back.

The wood stove had burnt right down, but Honour found a few coals and soon got the fire going again, and had water heating. We stripped Malcolm and spent the next hour sponging him down. Honour gave him an aspirin crushed in a little water and at last she was satisfied that his temperature was down far enough. We put a clean pair of pyjamas on him and I took him into bed with me. I had to change his pyjamas and the sheets again during the night because they were ringing wet with his perspiration, but he didn't wake. Thankfully he seemed fine when he finally woke the next morning, much later than his usual 5.30 am. I kept a close eye on him all day and he appeared to be all right, although not his usual boisterous self. I watched him for several weeks, but there was no recurrence of that frightening night. The doctor examined him on his next visit and told me that little boys are prone to high temperatures while teething. Thank heavens I didn't have any more boys to test out this theory. What I would have done if Honour hadn't been next door I don't know. I'd been so shocked when I read the thermometer that my mind had gone blank. The year was 1953 and Malcolm was just two years old.

We hadn't been back for very long when Mrs Absolom called in to see me. She wanted to know if I was interested in forming a ladies group to meet once a week in alternate women's houses for afternoon tea. I was quite agreeable and after visiting the other ladies she returned to say they were happy to meet each Wednesday. The first meeting was held in her house and each woman brought a plate. We all felt that we were well and truly country women so we decided to see if we could join the Country Women's Association in Katherine, and we thought that if we were to join the CWA we'd better have elected members. I became president, the schoolteacher, Helen Everleigh, became secretary, and Mrs Absolom became the treasurer, and we felt very proud of ourselves. We wrote to the CWA president, Mrs Shaw, but never received a reply. Nevertheless, we felt as though we belonged, even if we were not officially recognised at the time. Many years after I left VRD I saw in a local paper that a CWA group had been formed at Victoria River Downs, with many guests invited for the inaugural meeting. I had a chuckle to myself. Although not official, we had done that long before.

Next we decided to take up an offer from the Western Australian Government to pay freight on fruit for children in the outback – one piece per day per child. The fruit had to be ordered from Perth and was carried all the way on the MacRobertson aircraft which called every week at VRD. We sent a letter off and the scheme was soon in operation. Then Mrs Absolom had a clever idea. On our meeting days, all our husbands had been coming for their afternoon cup of tea and each husband always seemed to have one of the single men in tow. We decided that if they liked our cooking so much, maybe they'd appreciate some home cooking every weekend. At this time we enjoyed a weekly picture show which was held in the school every Saturday night. Mrs. Absolom suggested that we each make a cake on Saturday and offer them to the single men for their supper. The men thought this was a great idea and the ladies were rushed as soon as the pictures were over each week. With this project we were able to raise enough money to pay for the fruit, and from this time on every child had a piece of fruit every day – some feat in the bush at that time, I can assure you.

There were quite a few white children on VRD at this time. I had three, the Absoloms had three, and the Italian blacksmith had three, but only his two boys attended school. His daughter had to stay at home and help her mother. Their name was Magnoli and as Mrs Magnoli didn‘t speak any English we rarely saw her, and she was the only lady on the station who didn't attend our meetings. The Clearys had four children, the Parrys had two, and the Cornish family had three. This made a total of eighteen, most unusual I should think, for a station to have so many at that time.

Scott McColl went down to Sydney that year to be married and brought his lovely wife Mary home with him. She was a delightful girl and everyone came to love her. She was a trained nursing sister and soon took over this job, and fitted very well into the station life. We asked Mary to be our president at our next elections, and our children's fruit project rolled merrily on. Soon Christmas and the New Year came around and all the married staff were invited to the Big House to see in the New Year. This was Mary's first official party, and in fact the first to be held since Scott McColl had arrived, and what a great success it was. It was 2 am before George decided it was time to go home to bed. Goodness knows how much he'd had to drink as he'd been mixing beer and various spirits all evening, but he was well away. Even I was feeling very happy after several scotches, well drowned in plenty of water.

Never will I forget *that* New Year's Party. We arrived home and went to bed, and as usual George wanted sex. Drunk as he was, this time he found it difficult to perform and took considerably longer than the slow count to ten I usually made. Suddenly, for the first time in my life an exquisite feeling flowed through my body and I started to cry out – and George collapsed on top of me, laughing his head off. When this feeling was suddenly cut off I burst into tears with the shock. George rolled over onto his side of the bed and lay there giggling and laughing until he fell asleep, while I was left sobbing my heart out. At last I knew what sex and marriage should really be like and I couldn't believe that for four years I'd just been used for sex. It was very hard for me to face this unpalatable truth, but as far as I could see that was all I'd been married for.

To take my mind off things I decided I needed good physical exercise to tire me out, so once again I set about making myself a flower garden. It took me some time to get a bed dug because the soil was compacted, and I doubt if anyone had ever dug it up before. I left the hose running on the patch I'd selected and when it soaked in a little I got a mattock and made a border around my intended plot. I filled it with water again, and did so for a couple of days to let the water soak in as deep as possible. Then I got to work with a pick and turned the whole bed over. I asked George if a boy could bring me some manure from the yards and when it came I spread it around and dug it in, and broke the clods of dirt up thoroughly. Now my bed was ready.

I sent away to Coxes' store in Katherine for some flower seeds and these soon arrived. I'd made a big rectangular bed and I planted larkspurs in the centre, surrounded these with zinnias, then stocks, and phlox made the border. I smoothed some loose sand over the seeds and gave them a good watering, and sprayed the bed lightly every morning and evening until the seedlings came up. I wasn't quite sure at first which were weeds and which were flowers, so I waited until I was sure before beginning to weed the bed. From then on I watered the plot every afternoon as soon as the heat had gone out of the sun.

My flower garden was the prettiest on the station that year, and with no Aboriginals to do the hard work either. I had a house girl, of course, but with my three children she had enough to do keeping up with the washing each day, as well as the usual housework. Besides, I enjoyed my gardening. I always had ever since I was very small and mum gave me my own little patch to take care of.

While we were at VRD my grandmother died and I received a cheque from her estate. With some of this money I decided to buy a second-hand car so we'd be independent of station transport. I'd heard that the mail truck the contractors used between Darwin and Alice Springs was for sale, and decided to get it. It was an International tray-top utility with an engine from a three-ton truck, and it turned out to be an excellent buy. With a set of chains on the wheels it would go almost anywhere in the wet, and it was to serve us faithfully for some years.

In 1954 I became pregnant once again and towards the end of the year we decided that George would drive all of us down to Alice Springs, put the truck on the train, and my brother and his wife would meet the children and me at Port Augusta and drive the truck down to Adelaide. On the way down we stopped for lunch at Dunmarra, a roadside, ramshackle sort of country pub owned by Noel and Ma Healey. We asked if any lunch was available and Ma told us we could have sandwiches, and directed us to wait in an old bough shed about a hundred yards from the main building. We entered and sat down at a large roughly-hewn wooden table, with two long forms for seats.

The building had been gauzed in when it was first built, but the gauze was now hanging in tatters. George and I looked at one another and wondered just what would arrive for our lunch. After quite a wait Ma brought our food out, almost at a run, and I thought she must be conscious of the fact that we'd been waiting for some time, but I was wrong. She dropped the plates on the table and made off as fast as her legs would carry her, and the next minute we heard a strange sound of squealing and grunting, and a tribe of pigs came stampeding around the corner and made straight for us. We all jumped up onto the table, our appetites gone, and after a few hasty bites we threw the rest of our sandwiches as far away as we could and made a dash for the truck. Later we heard many funny stories about the Dunmarra pub and no matter how bizarre they seemed, after our experience there we were always inclined to believe them.

My eldest brother and his wife met me at Port Augusta as planned and he drove the truck down to Adelaide. There my youngest daughter, Erica, was born at the beginning of October 1954. This made four children and a miscarriage in five years of marriage, and I was determined I wouldn't have any more. Later George came down to drive us all back again. For this trip we bought a caravan and it was wonderful to not have to bother with swags. About half way between Port Augusta and Alice Springs we came to an outstation where we thought we'd stay the night.

Darkness had fallen but there were no lights in the homestead. A mob of cattle was drinking from the trough and they seemed very restless, and spooked when we drove up. I don't know what it was, but the place seemed quite eerie. Neither George nor I spoke and even the children were unaccountably silent. George swung the car away and we drove on for a few miles before pulling up to make camp. 'I didn't like the feel of that place,' said George. 'No, it certainly felt queer', I replied. It wasn't until we reached Alice Springs that I found out why we'd all felt so afraid there in the dark – we heard a murder had been committed there a few weeks before.

We left the caravan in Alice Springs because the rains had started and we knew it would be impossible to get it to VRD. We continued on to Newcastle Waters and took the Murranji Track to Montejinni. Because of the mud we had to use chains on the wheels all the way, and this made the journey much slower. Eventually we arrived at Dashwood Crossing to find the river in full flood, but George had sent word ahead that we were on our way and we could see a vehicle on the far bank, along with the old boat which I'd used to service the planes years before. I wondered how they were managing to do without it and thought they might have bought a new one while I was away, but later I learned that a new aerodrome had been built on the site of the old racetrack so the boat was no longer needed.

George swam across and brought the dinghy back, and then made a trip across with the luggage. Every now and then a large log would go swirling by in the current and I hoped none would come down while we were crossing because we'd probably sink if we were hit by one. When he came back we all climbed in. I sat on the back seat holding Erica who was two months old, while George sat in the middle facing me with eighteen months old Anne between his feet, and the two older children sat in the bow. We pushed off and were soon racing along with the current.

George was using the oars to direct us towards the far bank when to my horror one of them snapped in two. This happened when we were in mid-stream and the full force of the current swept us downstream at a furious pace. The thought flashed through my mind, 'Which one will I save?', a ridiculous idea considering I can only dog-paddle. It's doubtful I could've saved myself, let alone any of the children, but I guess in times of panic you don't always think logically. Thankfully, George managed to steer us to the bank with just the one oar. We'd been carried quite a way downstream, but I'd never been so thankful to find myself on solid ground. We walked back to the crossing and started for home, and it was a welcome relief to see the station lights. The next day big storms swept in and all the roads were impassable for weeks – we'd just made it.

The wet season that year, 1954, was a very heavy one – it rained for weeks on end. The Wickham River ran a banker and during the night, every now and then we'd hear a distant roar as parts of the riverbank caved in. Weeks later when the river had subsided to just a trickle we saw a large congregation of birds some miles up the river at the crossing, and decided to investigate. We drove up to the crossing, but couldn't get near it for the stench of rotting fish. The place was alive with kite hawks, crows, and even a pair of wedge-tailed eagles, all feasting on the carcases. About a month later we went back again to see what the birds had left, and found the whole crossing covered with fish bones. Thousands of fish had perished there and from the size of some of the jawbones some of them were monsters. If you put your fingertips together and make a circle with your arms, you'll have some idea of the size of the mouths of these jawbones. They probably came from 'old man' catfish, but whatever they were they were enormous.

We wandered around not saying very much, too stunned by what we were seeing. Later I recalled hearing the banks collapsing during the floods and I think this must have been the cause of the deaths. To have so many tons of red silt suddenly stirred into the water probably suffocated the fish, and the crossing had collected their bodies as the river subsided. I wondered just how many more had been swept away down the river and I also wondered just how old some of those fish were. They must have lived in the deepest parts of the permanent holes for many years to reach that size, until a freak of nature killed them.

PART 4

RETURN TO MT SANFORD

Things Had Changed

Scott and Mary McColl left VRD in the middle of 1955 and Scott's place was taken by Jack Quirk, a very experienced cattleman who'd worked for Vesteys for many years. Quirk arrived in September and he soon realised the mustering figures for Mt. Sanford had fallen since George left so he asked him to take over there again. As usual George came in and told me to pack up because we were leaving, but he wouldn't tell me where we were going. We left the next day, before I had time to say goodbye to any of the other women at VRD, and I soon realised we were headed back to Mt. Sanford.

There'd been some early storms, but the crossing was fordable and we had no trouble until we got to small a black soil plain between Gordon Creek homestead and the Wickham Gorge where we became badly bogged. As we ground to a halt we both opened our doors and the two elder children jumped down from the back. Getting bogged had become so commonplace that no one needed to say a word. George reached for the shovel and began digging the mud and slush from beneath the back wheel. I reached for the axe and with the two older children walked over to a stand of bushy saplings and began cutting them down. As fast as I cut them the children would drag them to their father to wedge under the wheels so they could get a grip in the dreadful mud.

We made it through the Wickham Gorge and soon came to a place where the road passed quite close to a lone tall tree on the top of a bare, stony hill. Over the years we'd watched a pair of wedge-tailed eagles nest here and they'd become so used to us that they never bothered to fly off as we approached. Suddenly George stopped. There were the two beautiful birds, both shot dead, the hen bird still sitting on the nest and her mate hanging from a branch. Why anyone would want to destroy such magnificent birds I don't know, because here all they lived on was wild game, and they certainly couldn't kill a calf. We never discovered who the culprit was.

Eventually we made it to Mt. Sanford. It had been quite a trip and I sometimes wonder how my children survived. Along the way little Erica's milk had to be made up from whatever water was available, and often this came from a gilgai, a small billabong formed in a depression on the black soil plains. Gilgais hold pure rainwater but can get a bit muddy sometimes from the cattle. I'd collect a billycan full from the deepest part I could reach, boil it up and then let the sediment settle before mixing it with powdered milk. Thankfully Erica thrived on it.

We received a tremendous welcome from the Aborigines when we arrived. I hugged all the girls and they exclaimed over the two new faces of Anne and the baby Erica whom they hadn't seen before. Many of them were in tears and they told me that the last missus had been very hard. They said that after they'd finished their usual jobs she'd give them any job she could think of, just to keep them busy. Sometimes she'd make them sweep the whole yard, other times she made them pick up and wash any pieces of rag lying about and when they were dry they'd just be thrown away.

The next day I walked around looking at all the changes and it was clear the girls hadn't been willing workers for the last missus. The gardens about the house that I'd worked so hard to get going years before were gone. The bananas and paw-paws had all died and only the plantains watered by the overflow from the tank were still there. Even the vegetable garden down by the creek was a sorry sight, with only the old water channels showing through a sea of weeds. I had no choice but to start again from scratch.

When we'd left Mt. Sanford George had put Moonlight into the stallion paddock where he thought she'd be safe, and two other horses old Jack McDonald had given me as a wedding present we'd sent to Charlie Schultz. When Moonlight didn't turn up in the muster George asked the boys if they knew where she was. Much to my dismay they told him the head stockman who took over after we'd left had tried to ride her and she'd bolted with him, so he shot her. I cried for my lovely mare and would've liked to have gotten my hands on her killer. What beautiful foals she might have thrown if she'd been left in with the stallion.

The fowls and ducks were gone too, and many of the goats had disappeared. They'd been left to themselves and not kept together in a herd, and this meant that many had strayed and become lost, or been killed by dingoes. None of the male kids had been castrated so one of George's first jobs was to attend to this. Castrating the goats made them grow nice and fat, and their meat made a welcome change from beef. We also sent away for a setting of eggs and Charlie Schultz lent me his chicken brooder. With this I successfully hatched and reared a couple of dozen chicks. The nights were cold at this time of the year so I made a coop for the chickens, with one end divided off with a piece of bag. At night I placed the old hurricane lamp in there with a piece of gauze wire wrapped about it to stop the chicks from getting burnt.

The next thing I had to do was get the girls to help me repair the fowl house. This had a galvanised iron roof with sides made from spinifex woven between strands of fencing wire. It made a cool shelter for the birds as it let the breeze through, but would stop any rain from blowing in. During our first years at Mt. Sanford the Aboriginal huts had been located down on the flat in front of the house about a quarter of a mile away, and most of them had been constructed in this manner. Since we'd left the whole camp had been moved up onto the hill behind the homestead, a stony area which must have been most uncomfortable for everyone. Gone were the cool grass huts with their iron roofs and in their place was a conglomeration of humpies made from bits of old roofing iron and branches.

The Aboriginal population had also changed. Big Alice and her family, including the two little part-coloured boys and an older part-coloured girl named Mildred, had moved to Humbert River. According to the girls, Alice had been told that Mildred would have to go to Darwin so they took themselves off to Humbert where she'd be safe, and Mildred was going to school there with several other children of mixed blood that Hessie Schultz had taken under her wing. Long Jack and Dolly (Wanyi) and their daughter Vera had moved to Wave Hill where Vera had married. Galloping Peter and my tribal sister May and her three children were still at Sanford, but her sister Bessie and her family had gone.

One of the old workers I really missed was our wood boy, old Jimmy Broken-tail. I asked about him several times over the years, but either the girls didn't know or they wouldn't say. He was a little hunched-up figure who seemed to walk from just the knees down and he'd been a great hunter in his young days, but he'd stolen another man's wife and she was the wrong skin category for him to marry. For this crime the old men of the tribe punished him by cutting him open and removing his kidney fat. Luckily for him he was found by the Wave Hill policeman, and the policeman's wife who'd been a nursing sister managed to save his life. From this time on he was a cripple, but he was a good man with an axe and kept the station supplied with wood for a number of years. During walkabout time Galloping Peter and Long May never attended the 'Big Sunday' ceremonies up in the sandstone country because their skin categories were incompatible and their marriage was illegal in the eyes of the elders of the tribe. Peter would have been well aware of what had happened to poor old Broken-tail Jimmy when he committed the same crime, and I expect that he was making sure that what happened to Jimmy didn't happen to him.

'Bullocky Bill' and Other Characters

While we'd been away at Mistake Creek a poddy calf had been raised at Mt. Sanford. 'Bullocky Bill' had been hand fed the best of every thing and had grown to an enormous size for his age. By the time we returned he was a very spoilt individual and a regular nuisance about the place. If he managed to get into the house yard on washing days he'd chew the sheets and clothes, ruining every thing. I tried to keep him locked in the horse paddock, but I suspect that the horse-tailer let him through with the horses when he mustered them up in the mornings because he always managed to turn up again. Once through the gate he would quickly turn up at the kitchen, stealing bread and being a general nuisance.

Anne liked to play on the back veranda where it was cool, usually by herself, with Topsy keeping an eye on both her and baby Erica. I was busy in the kitchen one morning when I heard piercing screams coming from the veranda. I rushed out to find Bullocky Bill under the lean-to, tossing his head and ripping the thatched roof with his enormous horns, and missing Anne's face by inches. I gathered her up just as the girls arrived on the scene. Topsy had only left the children for a moment to take the dirty clothes over to the laundry girls, but it was enough time for Anne to follow her and push the gate open, which Topsy hadn't latched properly. That was enough for me – Bullocky Bill had to go. George put him in the first mob of bullocks to leave the station, but he was so fat and lazy he couldn't be made to keep up with the mob, and returned in a few days. Everyone thought it a great joke but me.

A few weeks later I needed a killer. I picked up my ·22 rifle, walked up to Bullocky Bill, who was down by the vegetable garden, put the gun to his trusting head and pulled the trigger. I was sorry to have to kill him, but I knew no one else would do anything about him and I knew that once he was dead I wouldn't have to worry about the babies any longer. Well, I nearly had a riot on my hands! An old boundary rider named Fred Schull was there at the time and he declared that he wouldn't eat a bite of the meat, but later he ate everything I put in front of him. There were also a few remarks made in my hearing about hardhearted females, but I ignored them. Thankfully the episode was soon forgotten, although old Fred occasionally remarked on Bullocky Bill's absence when no one else was around. Apparently he never forgave me because when eventually he left I discovered that my old recipe book had a fistful of pages ripped out.

Fred Schull was a real character, a big lumbering bear of a man who spoke with a German accent. He'd lived in the area for many years and made his living doing contract work building yards and fences, and using a donkey team and a huge cumbersome dray made from bush timber. For a time he was employed on Wave Hill station grading the roads, but when the government began maintaining the roads this work fell through. He turned up at Sanford and was given the job of boundary rider. He could barely read or write and occasionally asked me to read letters for him which he received from his sister in Mt. Isa. Fred once told me he didn't trust banks and I discovered that he had a sugar bag nearly full of crown pieces which had long since been withdrawn as legal currency. Where he'd got them all from I don't know, and what became of them after he left us I don't know either. I think they must have been his life savings because he wouldn't use a bank, and I only found out about them when he gave me one for each of the children.

Fred's team of donkeys was fascinating to watch being worked. He had about twenty in his team and they all knew their places, so it didn't take too long for him to harness them up. Then he'd crack his whip and call, 'Gee up Captain, gee up Major', and off they'd go. All his commands were given to the two leaders and I never saw them make a mistake. When he wanted them to turn to the right it was 'Gee off Major', and to the left it was 'Way back Captain'. To halt the team he'd just call, 'Whoa'. Fred told me once that donkeys were very stubborn animals and if they decided they weren't going to work it was impossible to get them to move. He said that he'd even started a fire under the leaders once and they still refused to move, but I think he was trying to pull my leg with that one because he was usually very kind to animals. Others have told me that nothing can get donkeys to work once they've decided they've had enough. There's an old saying, 'as stubborn as a mule'. Well, a mule is half donkey so perhaps that's where their stubbornness comes from.

Old Fred once gave me a very old recipe book for making various forms of liquor. One time when the stock camp had left for the bullock muster and I knew I wouldn't see them for eight or nine weeks, I decided to make some hops beer. I'd just emptied a fifty pound flour drum so after getting Broken-tail Jimmy to smooth the rim, I set to work. I carefully boiled the hops, added the sugar and left it to brew for fourteen days. Then I added six cups of the chooks' wheat and left it for another ten days. Finally the big day arrived. I'd collected a dozen large bottles and corks, and after sterilising them in the kitchen oven I carefully strained the brew through a piece of muslin. I bottled the beer and stowed the bottles under the flour bags which were kept on a special wooden frame to keep them away from the termites.

Eventually the stock camp returned and one day while everyone was sitting having afternoon smoko there was a loud bang! 'My beer' I cried, and I rushed out to find that two bottles had exploded. Before I knew what was happening the remaining bottles were in the dining room, and I was being told it was no use to leave them to blow up. Needless to say there was no more work done that day and a very happy crew finally had their tea and collapsed into bed early that night. It must have done them all some good because everyone was happy and cheerful the next day. I don't know why, but I never tried to make any more beer, although I did make some apricot brandy for Christmas that year.

Health Scares

Whenever I was busy in the kitchen little Topsy was usually the one left in charge of Anne. She and all the other girls had endless patience with little children and completely indulged them. I never saw an Aboriginal child smacked and they had no discipline until the age of about eight or ten years, but once the early years were left behind their lot in life was a hard one. Late one afternoon as I was preparing tea, Topsy came rushing in to me. She was frantic and her speech was unintelligible. I managed to get only one word – kerosene. I flew across to the house to find Anne sitting on the floor gasping for breath. I snatched her up, up-ended her and smacked her back. A gush of liquid came out and I could smell kerosene.

Topsy had decided to fill the kerosene refrigerator so she filled some bottles with kerosene and left them on the floor while she went to get a funnel. Anne crawled after her and grabbed a bottle and took a swig. The poor little mite still couldn't get her breath. I frantically ran through my mind all the things I could think of that might help, but before I could do anything Anne suddenly took a deep gasping breath and began to cry. I was so relieved that I began to cry too. I called the Flying Doctor Service and was told to give her warm milk and to watch her closely for twenty-four hours – I sat up most of the night and they were the longest twenty-four hours I ever spent. As usual the stock camp was away and I was alone when this happened. The children always seemed to have a crisis when George was absent, and this made being on my own quite frightening.

I didn't see Topsy for several days. The girls said she was feeling 'big sorry' and would return to work when she felt better. I never mentioned the incident to her and in fact I never scolded her for her carelessness – I'd been too concerned with the baby at the time to say anything – but she obviously felt very badly about the whole affair. She disappeared soon after and was away walkabout until the following year, and she would never mind the children or work in the house again, but kept the men's quarters tidy and did their washing.

The next year Topsy's husband, Old Barney, died. Topsy and her fourteen year old son Bilgari left and we didn't see them for the next two years. When they returned Bilgari was taken into the stock camp and no one was prouder than Topsy.

That year the medical service did a survey and Bilgari was found to have leprosy. We were given tablets for him and out in the camp George saw that he took them each day, but the next time the stock camp came in Topsy and Bilgari disappeared into the bush. Later the girls told me that Bilgari had died: 'Him all swell up missus', they told me. Later I asked the doctor about this and he said Bilgari was probably one of the unfortunate few who were allergic to the tablets. At this time, unfortunately, very little was known about allergies and I presume that no one was expecting anyone to have any reaction from the tablets. I was horrified and to this day I feel very sad about this young boy's death. I never saw Topsy again and often wondered if she thought I gave her payback for nearly killing my baby. I sincerely hope she didn't.

I never felt comfortable about having to treat everyone in the bush, especially the first year at Mt. Sanford when there was no wireless. I was always conscious of my lack of medical training, and even when people only complained of a headache and asked for an aspirin I wondered if I was doing the right thing. Until you have the responsibility for everyone's health on your shoulders you don't realise just how much you've taken on. Everyone seemed to be so trusting in my abilities, but if only they'd known how *I* felt.

Late one night I got another fright. Merran called out to me and said she had a pain in her stomach. She was a bit hot so I took her into bed with me and she settled down and went to sleep. Once again I was woken by her cries of pain, but when I went to touch her, she begged me not to. I began to panic as I couldn't think what could be the matter with her. I called the Flying Doctor Base on the emergency signal several times and eventually received a reply from someone at Air Traffic Control in Cairns who said they would get a message through to Wyndham for me. I was amazed as Cairns was about 1000 miles away from me in the opposite direction from Wyndham. Presently the doctor came on the radio and after I told him about Merran he advised to watch her and give a report again in the morning.

Merran seemed to be much better in the morning but I was worried that the problem might reoccur. Over the radio the doctor advised that it was probably a case of infantile appendicitis which usually righted itself. I certainly wasn't very happy about the whole thing. It's very scary when you're on your own and don't know what to do for a child in extreme pain, as Merran was that night. Thankfully the doctor was right and it didn't occur again, but I continued to worry for quite a while.

When Erica was about nine months old I began to have health problems myself. I heard via the wireless that the doctor was to visit VRD, but for some reason not Mt. Sanford, so we packed the truck and made a quick trip down for me to see him. His diagnosis was that I had a retroverted uterus, which was very painful and needed surgery. The next morning I was flown to Katherine in the little Miles Gemini Flying Doctor plane, and arrived in time to catch the flight to Darwin. There, an English surgeon who was on loan from London did the operation. He was very good, and after the operation he told me it would be wise not to have any more children or I'd probably need to have the operation repeated to repair the damage. This made me more determined than ever not to have any more children.

Before I went to Darwin Vi Crowson at Montejinni offered to look after the children. I was worried that Erica might be a bit upset at my leaving so I put a dummy in with her things. She'd never used one before, but I thought it might comfort her if all else failed. Every time Vi gave Erica the dummy she'd throw it out of the cot, and Vi got tired of continually sterilising it so she threw it away. The Crowson's had three children, the oldest being Brian who was then in his early twenties, and he became very fond of Erica. When Vi threw Erica's dummy away he felt very sorry for her, and picked it up and began to carry it around in his jeans pocket. He'd take it out occasionally, look at it sorrowfully and say, 'Poor little Erica'. One day while out mustering he took a fall and landed on the dummy in his pocket, and this cut quite deeply into his leg. Needless to say the dummy was pitched far away into the scrub and no more was heard of 'poor little Erica'.

The Beginning of the Galah Sessions

The Royal Flying Doctor Service was run from the base at Wyndham in Western Australia, so they worked on a different time to the Northern Territory. This meant that our first session for the day started at 6 am. There were four main sessions when telegrams could be sent and received, and it was also common for the Wyndham operator, Greg Ryle, to pass on verbal messages from stations wanting to arrange a time to speak to their neighbours.

One day I received a message that I was wanted at the end of the 10 am medical session. I duly tuned in, and on came John Gordon. He went through a roll call of several stations in his district, but I was the only one in the Wave Hill police district. I remember Vi Crowson from Montejinni, Camille Fogarty from Auvergne and Enid Durack from Kildirk were some of those called. We spent a pleasant hour chatting to one another and it was arranged that we would do this at the same time each day, and so the famous 'Galah Session' came into being. I don't know who was responsible for the name, but I guess it was apt as the galah is the noisiest and most foolish bird in the bush.

I think the two most isolated women in the region must have been Enid Durack and myself because we rarely missed a session. Often we were the only ones to come on air and we'd have a great chat together, and what a Godsend it was. Over the years I only managed to see another white woman to talk to about two days in every six months. There were plenty of men to talk to when the camp was in, but men's talk is so different to woman's talk and after six months I really looked forward to talking about the things that interested me – not horse racing, cricket, tennis and work, which was about all I heard from the men.

Enid and I became great friends, swapping news and recipes, and one day she asked if I could send her children a pair of bantams. I had plenty because they breed so quickly, so the next time Alf Absolom passed through I gave him a pair to send on to Kildirk. On his next trip he turned up with a pair of cattle dog pups and some good banana suckers that Enid had sent. The pups were a blue heeler bitch for Merran, which she named Jingles, and a male black and white kelpie for Malcolm, which he insisted on calling Rusty. I tried to tell him this was a name for a red-coloured dog, but he was adamant, so Rusty it was. Within a few months the girls had brought me a young joey whose mother had been killed by one of the boys, two butcherbird chicks, a plains turkey chick and a tiny baby echidna. All survived except the echidna. I fed it on goats' milk through an eyedropper, but it was too young and I had to get George to destroy it. Later a kitten arrived from somewhere and the whole menagerie settled down well together. By this time the pups were half grown and slept back to back. The kitten slept curled up to Jingles' tummy, and the joey in the same spot with Rusty. The turkey chick (Turk-Turk) nestled into the white ruff around Rusty's neck and the two butcherbirds perched on a wire stretched above them.

When the first rains arrived grasshoppers hatched out and every day we'd give the Aboriginal children half a stick of nicki-nicki for a half a small jam tin of grasshoppers for George to feed to the now voracious 'Turk-Turk'. The supply tailed off after a couple of weeks as the children went on walkabout and from then on it was most amusing to see great big George, walking through the grass armed with a fly swat. Every time it came down, the grass behind him would wildly shake as little 'Turk-Turk' rushed forward for his meal. When the grasshoppers disappeared we weaned him onto fresh meat, and he did very well.

Eventually the butcher birds flew away and George took the dogs out into the camp, which left the homestead unprotected from the camp dogs. When Joey was about two years old the camp dogs killed her. I missed her badly as she'd been such good company about the house and would come when I whistled to her. The kitten also disappeared, probably sharing the same fate as Joey, but apart from making himself sick for a few days from trying to eat a lighted cigarette out of someone's fingers, Turk-Turk thrived. He slept under the lean-to at the back of the house and each morning as I left to go over to the kitchen he'd accompany me, and then continue on to the airstrip where he'd catch his breakfast.

One morning just at piccaninny daylight he took flight instead of walking. In the bad light his feet hit the top wire of the fence and he did about three complete somersaults before landing with a crash. I held my breath, sure that he'd broken a leg or wing, but he staggered to his feet, gave himself a shake and then went off for his breakfast. I never saw him try to fly from the house again. Eventually he got the mating urge and went bush. Years later one of the boundary riders on VRD said a turkey had come right up to him in his camp and taken the bread he was eating right out of his hand. It gave him quite a shock, but he'd heard tales of Turk-Turk and thought it must have been him. Once he'd mated, Turk-Turk never came back to the house again and I hope his trusting nature didn't later cause his death.

When the wet season was over I was having my usual morning talk to Enid Durack on the galah session when she mentioned that her vegetable seedlings were coming along nicely. I proudly replied that I'd already started to pick lettuce, silver beet and Chinese cabbage. I told her I always started my first seeds in a nursery bed covered with gauze, so they were ready to plant out as soon as the rains had finished.

The only garden produce we had all year round was paw-paw. I had about thirty trees once again which kept us well supplied with fruit, and at times I had to give some to the fowls because there were too many for the Aboriginal camp to eat.

About two weeks after this conversation I heard a vehicle approaching along the Wave Hill track. This turned out to be a truck driven by a bright young man who announced that at Wave Hill they‘d heard me tell Mrs Durack about my vegetable garden, so he'd been sent over from Wave Hill station to get some. I was staggered to say the least! Wave Hill homestead was built on a limestone ridge similar to Mt. Sanford, but they had ample staff and several hundred Aboriginals to make a large garden down on the Victoria River if they wished. In fact, an old Chinese had kept a garden there for many years. I thought of all the hours of hard labour my girls had put in to the garden when I came back from Mistake Creek. They'd spent hours carrying soil and manure from the yards in buckets hung from a yoke across their shoulders and it had taken them several weeks to make it ready for planting once again. It was hot tiring work, but they did it cheerfully because they knew that they'd get their share of all we produced. My poor little garden was only large enough to keep Mt. Sanford in a steady supply. 'What a cheek', I thought! Well, I wasn't going to strip my garden for them.

I apologised to the young man who I think was the Wave Hill mechanic, and explained that my garden was very small and only a few things were ready to pick each day, but he could have all the paw-paw that I had. He looked disappointed, but philosophically took what I gave him and went on his way. This brought home to me the fact that nothing anyone said on the wireless was private. Every word was heard for hundreds of miles around, so from then on I was always careful of what I talked about with Enid.

When the vegetable garden died at the end of the wet season I began to worry about the children not getting a proper diet. There were still a few paw-paws, but no vegetables. One afternoon they came up from the creek with the girls and I gave them their tea, but nobody seemed very hungry. I began to worry all the more and told Erica she had to eat her tea. She looked up at me with a pitiful expression and said, 'Me full up belonga bingie, me full up belonga yow (fish)'. I was stunned! Apparently the girls had spent the afternoon fishing and grilled the fish on the coals, and I discovered that as well as catching fish the girls would gather bush tucker such as melons, wild onions, roots and bush cucumbers, all of which they shared with the children. I looked at their little faces shining with health and blessed those girls. May really did mean it when she declared she was part-mother to my children. The rest of the whites may have felt the loss of the vegetable garden, but my children certainly didn't.

Learning From the Aborigines

Over time I began to learn a little about the Aboriginals' beliefs and customs, and their use of the native plants in the area. One plant they used was the pandanus tree which grows throughout the tropical region of the far north. It has fronds that grow in a spiral around the trunk and their edges are covered with very sharp spines. The girls would gather fresh leaves and leave them to soak in a springs for a few days. Then they'd pull off the outer barbed edges and tear the remainder into long strips which they'd weave into string dilly bags. When the pandanus fruit forms it looks something like an extra large pineapple, and it ripens into a yellow, orange or a very bright red. It can be broken into sections and the Aboriginals told me that each section contains an edible seed and also that the base of each section can be chewed, but is very 'cheeky' (hot). I never fancied trying any.

Another tree the Aboriginals used was what they called a 'sandpaper' tree. This has hard leaves with the undersides very rough like sandpaper, and they used these to smooth their wooden artefacts. Each leaf wouldn't last long but there were plenty more on a tree. Once I came upon the girls smoking what looked like small cigarillos, or little black cigars. They told me they were the roots of the freshwater mangrove which grew along the banks of creeks. When they were out of 'nicki-nicki' the girls would dig into the banks for these roots and collect those about as thick as a little finger. The roots were unusual in that they had a little hollow running up the centre. The girls would light one end and smoke it like a cigarette but when I tried one it burnt my tongue, which made the girls laugh.

Talking about tobacco reminds me of how the Aboriginals used their ration of nicki-nicki. Each of them possessed a small tin of very fine grey ashes which they gathered very carefully from the fireplace. This ash was made from a certain type of bark that burnt down into a very fine, almost white ash. A small piece of nicki-nicki was chewed until it was softened. Then it was rolled in the ashes and kneaded into a ball that was about half tobacco and half ashes, and this was placed in the pouch of a cheek where it was always quite noticeable. The first time I saw this I thought some of them had deformed jaws, but soon learnt what it was. When the owner had had enough it was removed and placed behind an ear or given to someone else. I've often seen one Aboriginal walk up to another with a hand outstretched. The person with the ball would take it from behind their ear and pass it over, and the two would then go about their business. I often used to wonder just how many times one ball of 'nicki' was passed on during the course of a day.

The first piece of genuine Aboriginal art I ever saw was an ironwood shield that belonged to Jimmy Broken-tail. It was very strong and heavy and I've never seen another like it. It was about two and a half feet long and made from a straight branch about six inches in diameter. One side was perfectly flat and the other was rounded. On the flat side a hole had been gouged out in the centre to form a handhold. As far as I could see there were no marks of any tools being used – the hole seemed to have been carefully burnt out. The rounded face was carefully etched in very fine detail with little sections of various animals and lines. Jimmy was very proud of this shield and told me he'd made it himself when he was a young man. I think it reminded him of when he was a strong young hunter, before the old men crippled him.

The coolamons the women used were also works of art. These were made from the trunk of a small tree or a large branch. They were about two and a half feet long and about one foot at the widest part, and the ends were roughly tapered. The centre of the log was gouged out and those I saw were made with white mans' tools. The women always carried the very small babies in them. They'd lay them on a bed of soft grass or leaves, and when they were soiled the lining was changed with a fresh lot. Sometimes they used old pieces of rag instead.

One afternoon the girls were sitting in the shade of the beef house having their smoko, and I noticed a little willy wagtail flitting amongst them catching the flies that always gathered whenever there was any food about. He danced around, busily wagging his little tail and obviously enjoying his own smoko. It dawned on me that none of the girls had spoken for some time which was most unusual, and I began to worry there might be a fight brewing. The girls' fights were awesome affairs with the combatants standing face to face with nulla nulla's in their hands. The aggrieved party would have the first hit and then stand while the other had her turn. Their weapons would alternately be used as a club or a defensive shield, and the usual injury from their fights was a smashed finger or two which I'd be expected to cure.

I went across to investigate, but when I got to the girls there didn't seem to be any ill feeling amongst the group, which puzzled me even further, and when Dolly looked up and anxiously whispered, 'No talk missus', I was even more mystified. Then Dolly rose to her feet, took my arm and led me away from the silent group. Pointing to the busy willy wagtail she said, 'You see that one dicky-bird missus? 'Im prop'ly cheeky bugger, 'im all about listen to talk-talk belonga we, then 'im go tell 'im lies, make big trouble belonga we'. 'Okay, Dolly', I replied, and went back inside. To me willy wagtails were friendly, cheeky little birds and their call of 'sweet pretty creature' was a welcome change from old 'Jim Crow', 'carking' in the bloodwood tree down by the gate, but no way would those girls talk and gossip amongst themselves while one was about. They believed it would listen and spread malicious gossip about them to others.

East of Mt. Sanford homestead there were two creeks which met about half a kilometre from the house. One ran past the bottom of the vegetable garden and there was a deep hole there where the girls spent most of their spare time after lunch. This was where they taught my children to swim. Years later Merran rescued some young Aboriginal boys who were trying to ride a log in a flooded river, so I guess they had the Mt. Sanford girls to thank for first teaching her to swim.

When the children were down at the waterhole I could hear them from the house, and Merran told me many years later that Erica was a terrible nuisance. She loved the water so much that she'd walk straight off the bank into the water. This was before she could swim, so Merran spent most of her time dragging her out. I was horrified to learn of this, but on reflection I guess the girls kept a good eye on them and none of the littlies would have been in any danger. In their eyes she enjoyed it, so nothing must interfere with that. They must just watch more closely. Aboriginals love children and would rarely stop them from doing anything which gave them pleasure, unless it was likely to hurt them. I'd consider it dangerous for a two year old child to jump into a six foot deep pool when she couldn't swim, but they obviously considered her quite safe while they all watched her. All the children at Mt. Sanford learnt to swim at a very early age and never seemed to have any fear of water. By the time she was three, Erica could easily beat me at swimming and all of them usually kept an eye on me as I dog-paddled along.

A kilometre from the house ran the second creek, a little larger than the first. There, two rock holes were fed from springs, and never dried up. There were rock cod in these holes, and when I first arrived George took me fishing there. In the hot weather I'd often go there in the late afternoons for a swim and to cool off just before tea. Later I learnt that this area was a 'Sunday Ground' and was tabu to women, so I never went there when the stock camp was home and I didn't go fishing there either.

When I walked past the children's beds one morning I noticed bits of old cigarette papers from butts under Malcolm's bed. I wondered what he'd been doing with them, fully expecting the worst. I kept my eye on him as he played about the men's quarters that morning, and later I asked him what the papers were doing under his bed. He gave me a sheepish look, then a mischievous grin, and told me that he and his little friend Rahbi had smoked a cigarette they'd made from the butts they'd collected. I shuddered, and gave a quick thought about how as a five-year-old I'd joined my sisters in raiding my father's tobacco jar, rolled the pipe tobacco in toilet paper and had a quiet smoke all those years ago. Quietly I explained to Malcolm that he and Rahbi could gather the butts from around the men's quarters, but he should give them all to Rahbi so that Rahbi could give the tobacco to his mother. I reminded him that May was always very good to him and his sisters, always giving them a share of any bush tucker she gathered for her family, and it would be a nice way in which to say thank you to her for this.

After this I often saw the two children busily gathering cigarette butts, but I never saw any more evidence that he was using them himself and I presumed that he'd taken my words to heart. I'm sure that if I'd tried to explain to Malcolm that it was unhygienic he wouldn't have listened, but he was a kind little boy and was willing to give his share away because he understood that May gave him so many of the native foods he really enjoyed. Strange to say he never really became interested in smoking when he grew up.

George came down from the yards one day looking completely stunned. He asked me if I'd noticed the lack of Aboriginal children around a certain age and I said I had and that I thought it most peculiar. 'I've discovered the reason', he said. While working that day one of the Aboriginal men about thirty-five or forty years of age urinated by the stockyard fence. George noticed his actions were unusual and asked what was the trouble. The man showed him how his penis had been shortened and a slit cut in the underside of the foreskin. And how the urine dribbled through this hole. He said at one time only all boys were treated this way at their initiation ceremony but he did not know why.

Judging by the age of the boy, he would have undergone this rite in the early 1920s, but why the old men of the tribe had decided to take this drastic action I don't know. Considering the operation was probably done with primitive tools, with no anaesthetic and only ashes for sterilising the wounds, the mind boggles. I later read that a Native Affairs Officer visiting all the stations in this area was amazed to discover that there were only seven children born in the past ten years, and recorded on the station books. Some concern was expressed by the station owners that if this continued there'd be a lack of native workers in the future. Years later I learned from a doctor that this procedure was a common and widespread practice at one time, but it didn't inhibit the ability to father children at all, so why there were so few children being born I don't know.

Each year as soon as the rains had renewed the land and all the bush tucker had grown and ripened, the Aboriginal camp would become restless. This was walkabout time when Aborigines for miles around would gather for sacred ceremonies and get the chance to see relatives perhaps not seen for several years, or to enter into marriage contracts. George would negotiate as to who would remain behind while the rest went walkabout, but I think the boys probably decided among themselves who would stay behind, giving George a few choices but making sure that those who needed to attend the ceremonies were free. Two married men and their families usually stayed at the homestead. This gave George the help he needed with the early stages of the horse breaking, and two girls to help me in the house and kitchen.

At the end of the walkabout one year, the Aboriginal children returned with heads full of lice. I knew nothing about it until one day when I washed my youngest daughter's hair. She was just two years old with long fair curls, and the only remedy I could think of was kerosene. This did the trick and I gave a sigh of relief, but then I noticed masses of eggs clustered along the hair close to the scalp. There was no chemist round the corner, so a drastic remedy was called for. I sat her on the table and proceeded to shave her head. A few tears fell with the curls, but I consoled myself with the thought that it would grow again, and it did of course, but as straight as candles – all the curls were gone! George was horrified when he saw his little darling as bald as a badger, and we had to tell the other children not to laugh or tease the baby or they'd get the same treatment. It worked. There were many horrified faces and whispered comments among the girls when they saw what I'd done, and later I saw them cuddling her with tears running down their faces as they rocked her in their arms, but they never again brought head lice back to the station.

Whenever the cold weather arrived the personal hygiene of the girls deteriorated. A heavy musky odour hung about them and because of this I'd tell them to be sure and 'bogey' while they were down at the creek, but this did no good. Because of this odour, one day I sent one of the house girls to change her dress. I watched her go to the laundry, remove all her clothes, put the top one she'd just removed on again first, then the others all went on top. Finally the penny dropped. The girls were wearing all their dresses all the time because they were cold, and it really was very cold, especially at night. Each morning they'd rearrange their dresses so that the one on top would appear to be clean. And so it was as far as dirt and stains were concerned, and although their body odour was most noticeable, I never complained after that. As long as they presented themselves with a clean dress each day, that was good enough for me.

They must have *really* felt the cold on washday when they had to strip and wash everything, and as soon as the clothes were dry they'd put the whole pile back on again. They were all given woollen jumpers each year, but I very seldom saw one being used. I never enquired what they did with them, but perhaps they gave them to their bush relatives or the men took them all for use in the stock camp. How miserable they must have been before the Europeans gave them clothes and blankets.

Stock Camp Cooking and the End of My Truck

The old mail truck I'd bought in 1953 served us faithfully for a number of years. It came in handy to recharge the battery for our wireless, and George sometimes made use of it in the stock camp. It also enabled the children and some of the girls and me to occasionally join the stock camp. On these visits I enjoyed being camp cook and soon got used to the routine. Water for camp use was kept in large canteens which were always in pairs so that one could go on each side of a packhorse. They were a good substitute for a seat when they were stood on their ends.

I also mastered the use of Bedourie ovens. These are round iron containers with a flat bottom and flat tight-fitting lids which double as frying pans. They usually came in a set of three that fitted neatly inside each other to make them easy to carry, and they were used to cook anything – roast dinners, stews, and cakes or bread. They have large handles to make them easy to move, and this was done with two pieces of fencing wire with hooks at one end and joined together with a small piece of chain at the other. The hooks fitted into the handles and the ovens and lids could then be lifted and shifted as required.

It took me a while to get the hang of using them. It's a case of knowing just what quantity of hot coals are needed to cook each item without burning it. With bread, for instance, once the dough is kneaded and placed in the camp oven it's necessary to build up the fire to be sure there are enough hot ashes and coals for when the bread had risen sufficiently to cook. A hole is dug near the fire, large enough for the camp oven to be lowered into it with just the top showing. A shovel full of hot ashes and coals are placed in the bottom of the hole, and then the oven is placed on top and a good shovel full of hot ashes placed on the lid. After fifteen minutes or so, these are scraped off and the lid carefully lifted to check the progress of the bread. Then the lid is replaced and recovered with hot ashes to complete the cooking. With practice it becomes easy to gauge the amount of coals that should be placed in the hole, and how much to put on the lid. I loved camp oven bread because it always had a lovely brown crust all over. Sometimes I made fruitcake and whenever I did the boys would have big grins on their faces when they came up for smoko.

After a few years of station work the old truck began to look a little bit shabby, so I decided to give it a coat of paint. I got some paint from Katherine and applied it in my spare time, and the next time George came in from mustering I proudly showed him my efforts. Shortly afterwards we had a visitor, George Lewis, a drover on his way to Wave Hill station with his plant. In the 1950s the droving game was becoming mechanised and as well as horses George Lewis had an old Landrover to carry his gear. This was only the second four-wheel-drive vehicle that I'd seen. The first was a Power Wagon Scott McColl had sent up after he'd gone south to get married, and it caused quite a stir at the time.

One morning after breakfast George asked if I'd like to go for a ride as he wanted to check a waterhole over in the hills. I hadn't been for a horse ride for some time so I was delighted to go. We had a very pleasant morning and arrived back in time for lunch, but as I walked to the house to change my riding gear I saw my lovely utility was gone! In its place was George Lewis's Landrover. I was furious! I knew then I'd been taken for a ride in more ways than one, but there was no point in making a fuss. I knew my truck was nearly to Wave Hill by this time so I held my tongue. I couldn't help reflecting on just how many times we'd crossed the continent in the old truck. I think we must have seen the so-called 'dead heart' in all its guises, from bleak dusty desert to a garden paradise, but as far as George was concerned he was the head of the family and could do as he pleased with my property.

For some years the Aboriginal workers had been paid a small allowance and whatever they earned was held in trust for them by the government. One day I heard on the radio that a hawker was coming to Mt. Sanford and when I told the Aboriginals they'd be able to buy things for themselves from a travelling storeman there was great excitement. They wanted to know if they had any money and I assured them that the office down at VRD had their money and they'd be allowed to buy whatever they liked. The hawker's name was Syd Hawkes.

Syd had a large truck set up as a travelling store so the Aboriginals could buy all kinds of things other than what the station store had supplied for years. They didn't handle any actual money. First Syd got a list from the office with everyone's names and how much money was held in trust for them, and then he'd sell them goods up to that amount. I never saw the Aboriginals so excited! They bought new dresses, at last with a bit of shape to them, there were R.M. William's brightly-coloured shirts everywhere, and that night there was a big corroboree down at the camp.

Syd and his wife Thelma later set up a store at Top Springs and did very well there. This was at the junction of roads which led to Wave Hill, VRD and Newcastle Waters, and they were soon doing a roaring trade. Top Springs is interesting for another reason. It was where one of the famous scenes from 'The Overlanders' was filmed by Charles and Elsa Chauvel. The scene was a herd of cattle supposedly perishing of thirst and rushing into a waterhole, and it looked very dramatic in the film.

Our Last Year at Sanford

In 1957 the first truck of the year brought us three new ringers and I mean *new*. One was a fair-haired boy with a flattop haircut which apparently was the latest thing in the big cities. The other two were cousins, Johnny and Keith. All three were from Sydney so they were immediately christened the 'Kings Cross Ringers', although they were really only raw jackeroos. Allan Griffiths, the part-coloured boy who'd been born at the head station and lived all his life in the Aboriginal camp also arrived. I was asked to help him to fit in and learn to live as a white. They all went out on the first mustering round, and by the time the stock camp came back six weeks later the Kings Cross Ringers had become quite good riders.

When the stock camp was in I never seemed to have time to stop and take a breath. I had to get up at four o'clock every morning to work on the bread, and have breakfast ready before daylight when the men started work. Then I had to produce a cooked morning smoko and the usual cold meat and salad for lunch, although sometimes I made pickled ox tongue or set a rare tin of salmon and fresh tomatoes in gelatine aspic for lunch. As well as supervising the meals being cooked for the Aboriginals I had to somehow find time to do the children's correspondence lessons and make a three course dinner at night. To finish off my day I had to set the bread at 10 pm, after which I'd fall into bed too tired to think.

The morning after everyone came in from the muster I was busy in the kitchen when I heard the truck start up. I never thought anything of it, but when nobody turned up for lunch I asked the kitchen girls where the boss had gone. To my surprise they replied, 'Boss, 'im and all about bin go along VRD, missus'. I just couldn't believe that George would go off without a word to me. I was very upset, but tried not to let the girls see it. How I would've loved to have seen my friends at VRD for a chat, even if only for a short time. George must've known this, and I could only conclude that taking the children and me was just too much of a bother for him.

The truck returned the next day and George organised a muster of the horse paddock so that everyone could get a fresh lot of horses for the next round of mustering. When each of the men was allocated his mounts he was set to shoeing them up in the old branding yard. Each man caught his horse, tied it to the rails of the fence and shod it, tying a set of hopples around its neck as he finished with it. Then he'd then go and catch another horse out of the mob. I don't know just how it happened, but the boy with the flat-top went into the mob and got kicked in the stomach. They brought him down to the house and I got all the information for a medical session over the wireless – his pulse, respiration and general condition. Because there was no sign of bleeding I was advised to keep him in bed for at least a week, as rest was all he needed.

A few days later he produced a perfect set of hoof prints in a bruise, but he refused to stay in bed. It annoyed me that he was supposed to be resting in bed but was never in it except at meal time. Then he'd hastily put himself back to bed and wait for me to bring his meals to him. In exasperation one lunch time I told him if he was well enough to walk around he could sit up for his meals with everyone else. A few days later Alf Absolom arrived and Flat-top went away with him. I would've tried to stop him if I'd known because the road was very rough, especially in a five-ton truck. I heard later that he got as far as Gordon Creek outstation, where he collapsed. When he recovered he started work there and never returned to Sanford, but he wasn't missed because he had a bad habit of 'acquiring' small items like tins of tobacco, pocket knives, and other things from other peoples' swags. This was considered a dreadful crime in the bush because a man's swag was his castle.

When the shoeing was finished George organised a supply of stores for the stock camp. The next morning everyone packed up and just as they were leaving George announced that I was to have all Merran and Malcolm's clothes ready in four weeks' time, as they were going to Halls Creek to attend the Australian Inland Mission School. I started to protest, but was just ignored and left standing, my heart in my mouth with shock. I burst into tears and took no notice as the stock camp left. All that day the girls were very quiet. They knew I was upset at something the boss had said to me, but they didn't ask any questions. In their own way they did all they could to show me little kindnesses, and to let me know that they cared for me.

George must have considered that my teaching the children was too much for me as I was always very tired by the time I went to bed, but I'd much rather have had the children with me. After all, he was away in the camp for six or eight weeks at a time, and only home for a week or ten days in between. To my mind the children were my main priority and the place was very lonely and empty without them once the stock camp left. The next time the stock camp came in the first thing George did was to take Merran and Malcolm off to VRD where he put them on a plane for Hall's Creek, all on their own – they were just six, and seven and a half years old. Every time I tried to talk to George he'd just walk away without answering. It broke my heart to see the children go, but there was nothing I could do, so I hugged and talked gaily to them as they left because I didn't want to make it more difficult than it already was. They both seemed so bewildered, poor mites. I didn't see them again until they came home before the rains started the next wet season. The next year Bob and Ethel Nelson offered to have them at VRD to live with their daughter, Barbara. Bob was the overseer and Ethel was the new schoolteacher. Once again I was not consulted, it just happened, and although they were not far away this time I still missed them very much.

I thought a great deal about the whole situation as soon as I was on my own and came to the conclusion that the children and I were always secondary to George's wishes, and that he thought only of himself. Even when he was home I hardly saw him as he spent all his spare time over in the men's quarters. After dinner each night I'd take a book and read until bedtime, or on bread nights until it was time to set the dough. Sometimes I'd have fallen asleep by the time George came to bed but it never mattered to him if I was asleep or not, tired out or not – he always woke me for the nightly sexual ritual. George would come to bed, get on top of me and work busily for a short time. It would last about as long as it took me to slowly count to ten under my breath, then he'd give a huge sigh and collapse on top of me, before rolling over to his side of the bed and within a few minutes be softly snoring. I knew there was something more to this ritual, but George would never talk about sex and I was abysmally ignorant, and I soon began to hate the thought of it.

I couldn't understand why after setting the bread I could go to bed feeling absolutely exhausted, but after George went to sleep I'd be wide-awake and unable to sleep. Many a night I'd walk around the house, sometimes until 2 o'clock in the morning, wondering just what was wrong with me. Then I had to get up at 4 am! I began to suspect the reason George had married me in the first place was so that he didn't need to bother about Aboriginal girls any more, and this meant that relations between him and the Aboriginal men were much more stable. There were no more episodes of everyone disappearing overnight as there had been before we were married. And to think I'd laughed with everyone about Jack Liddell and his troubles!

Later in the year George decided we'd go to the Wyndham Races so we packed up the truck and set off, with the Kings Cross Ringers and Griffo on the back. Merran and Malcolm were in school at Halls Creek so I only had Erica and Anne in the front with me, and on the way through Gordon Creek we picked up Gerry Woods. We took the road through Jasper Gorge to Timber Creek, then west to the Kununurra Research Station and on to Wyndham. I hadn't been back there since Anne was born and I asked George if we could make a detour to see Merran and Malcolm at Halls Creek, but he said no.

Soon we found Charlie and Hessie Schultz camped by the racetrack so we made our camp near them. Charlie had several Humbert River horses running, and on the last day he asked if I'd do him a favour and ride his horse 'Snowy' in the Ladies' Race. I wasn't very keen, but eventually he persuaded me to help him out. The time for the race arrived and I mounted up and took my place in the line-up. Next to me was Maggie Lilly on a big black stallion which she was having trouble controlling. The starter dropped the flag, and I dug my heels into Snowy and he leaped forward.

The next thing I knew the black stallion hit Snowy amidships while he had his fore feet off the ground. Poor Snowy nearly fell and cannoned into the horse next to him, which probably kept him on his feet. I lost the offside stirrup and just managed to stay on by grabbing his mane. For the next hundred yards I was fighting to find the stirrup which was flapping and bouncing madly about. Eventually I managed to slip my foot back in and a very shaken horse and rider pulled up last.

Not long afterwards Maggie came to find me and apologised for the mishap. She explained that she hadn't wanted to ride the stallion, but her husband had insisted. I accepted her apology because I well knew what it was like to have a domineering husband. At least that experience taught me one thing – it made me realise the danger of riding in races when you have a young family dependent upon you, and I never rode in a race again.

There was a dance on that night but I didn't think I'd be able to go because I couldn't leave the children on their own. However, Hessie had an Aboriginal girl to take care of her two little girls, so she kindly offered to get her to take care of my two as well. The dance was most enjoyable, and I turned in about midnight. It was difficult trying to wash off the bull dust in a small basin of cold water before getting into my swag, but I managed it. The next day we packed up and headed for home.

By this time the bullock muster was over and George took the camp out into the hilly country south-west of the homestead to begin the calf muster. As usual, the girls and I settled down for a few weeks' peace and quiet. One mid-morning I saw a rider coming in and I thought that George must be sending a message in for something. It turned out to be Johnny, one of the Kings Cross Ringers, and he said he'd come in for a 'cuppa' as he was quite close to the house. I told him he'd better have his lunch as well and let his horse have a spell until late afternoon as it looked a little weary. He agreed and after lunch went to sleep on his bunk. I had my suspicions that he'd become lost and that I'd better keep him busy until someone turned up for him. Sure enough, just at sundown Griffo arrived, very irate, and berated Johnny for not doing as he'd been told to do if he ever got lost.

When they were out mustering George had told the Aboriginals to keep an eye on Johnny as he had absolutely no sense of direction. When he started to stray one of them would ride to where Johnny could see him, and by keeping the boy in sight Johnny would get back to where he was supposed to be. Unfortunately no one had seen him disappear this time so he'd become hopelessly lost. When he didn't turn up at the dinner camp, George sent Griffo to back-track him. He'd followed him all the previous afternoon and all the next day until he finally found him back with me. Johnny's tracks showed that he'd made two complete circles and visited the same waterhole three times before he finally recognised Mt. Sanford in the distance, and made for it.

No wonder Johnny was looking for a 'cuppa' – he'd gone without food for a day and a half! Poor Griffo had been a full *two* days without food, and from hunger or relief he really gave poor John a dressing down. He finished his tirade with the best piece of advice anyone lost in the bush can get – once you've found water, *stay* there. If Johnny had only stayed at the waterhole he would've been found the first afternoon. I knew both their horses could do with a good spell so I prevailed upon Johnny and Griffo to have a good meal and a good night's sleep, and leave first thing after breakfast. The fire was going when I got up next morning and they were both gone, so I guess they got their own breakfast.

Shortly after this episode, George asked me if I'd like to take a ride with him to Chamber's Rockhole. The rains hadn't begun yet so surface water was getting scarce and George knew that a mob of brumbies was running in this area so he wanted to see if any station horses were with them. We started out early in the cool of the morning and arrived at the rockhole in time for lunch, but didn't make tea as the horses would smell the smoke. Instead we settled down among the rocks to wait.

About three in the afternoon we heard the clicking of hooves among the rocks and down below us appeared a beautiful stallion. We were down wind from him, but his instincts told him that something was different and he stood pawing the ground and tossing his head. Maybe he could sense our horses tied up under the trees behind us, but eventually he walked to one of the sandy depressions in the creek bed and began pawing out the damp sand to make it a little deeper. After a while we could see a little pool of water forming in the hole. After sniffing it, he finally took a drink and the rest of his herd came down to join him. They spread out over the area and soon deepened several of the depressions for themselves. It was wonderful to see these wild creatures digging for water in the sand where most people would probably pass by and never suspect that water was available. Suddenly the stallion threw up his head and within minutes there was not a horse in sight.

George was very interested in the stallion. He thought he looked like bloodstock and wondered if it could be the Wave Hill stallion which had disappeared some years previously. Rumour had it that Charlie Schultz had taken the horse, but he strenuously denied this. According to Charlie he'd sent three brood mares in season over to Owen Cummings, the horse master at Wave Hill, with the request that they be put to a stallion. Owen agreed to allow the mares to stay in the paddock for a couple of days to take pot luck as to whether they were serviced or not. When the fellow who took the mares to Wave Hill returned with them he also had one of the stallions in his plant. Charlie would have nothing to do with the horse and told the man, Arthur Grace by name, to return it at once before it was missed. It was possible that Arthur got cold feet and dropped it off in the wild country on Mt. Sanford, and if so the foals running with the brumby mares should make good stock horses.

George began to make plans to trap the brumbies late the following year when the surface waters would again be low. It was too late to start this year as it would take several weeks to build trap yards and to fence off any other waters in the area, and we were expecting the rains to start any day. As it turned out George never got the opportunity to try his luck and the progeny of these horses are probably still roaming the wild country around Chamber's Rockhole.

Leaving VRD

A few weeks after we'd gone to the rockhole I heard a motor vehicle coming along the track from the direction of Wave Hill. This turned out to be Ron Ryan, the District Welfare Officer from Katherine, who was making his annual check-up of his district. Ron was a kind man, well liked by all who knew him, and he always tried to do his best for the Aboriginals in his area. On his rounds he checked all the station records and talked to the Aboriginals to see if they had any complaints. I left him to talk to the girls and the people down in the camp while I prepared lunch. He soon returned to the house and asked if *I* had any complaints, which I thought was rather strange. After all, it was the Aboriginals he was supposed to be concerned with, not the whites.

Ron asked me if the rations had been reduced and if we now had enough. Living at Mt. Sanford under Jack Quirk's regime was entirely different from when Magnussen was manager. Quirk cut back on the stores, and although there was enough to go round if you were economical there was no surplus to allow the Aboriginals much more than the usual bread and beef, with occasional jam and golden syrup. None of the customary vegetable seeds arrived either so I'd arranged for some to be sent out from Katherine, but as these took about six weeks to arrive my garden was late that year. I didn't blame Jack Quirk for the cutbacks, but we really missed not having any fresh potatoes or onions. I could understand that they weren't very economical because by the time they arrived they'd be badly bruised, and many of them already rotten.

I told Ron about there'd been cutbacks, but that the Aborigines were still receiving the Government rations to which they were entitled as well as fruit and vegetables from the station garden, which most stations wouldn't provide. I just couldn't give the Aboriginals all the extras I'd been used to giving them. He then queried whether there was less tonnage being carted from Adelaide than there had been when I was working in the VRD store, and I told him I had no idea. The questions kept coming. Next he asked me if I was happy at Mt. Sanford and I truthfully replied that I missed my two older children very much, even though they were now boarding at VRD with Mrs. Nelson. I told him I often felt that life was rushing by and leaving me behind. In Adelaide I'd been accustomed to reading the daily papers and in my small way had kept up with events of general interest, and on Saturday nights I'd go to the pictures and watch the latest newsreels. Now I was living in a backwater and except for my books and my Womens' Weeklies, my knowledge of Australian and world affairs was very limited. I guess that the isolation was getting to me.

Ron told me that George had a very good reputation in the cattle industry and the position of station manager had become vacant at Beswick station only 100 miles from Katherine. This was a station run on behalf of the Aborigines by the newly formed Department of Social Welfare. Ron said he would recommend George for the position if he wanted it. I thanked him for his interest in us and he left that afternoon and went to VRD. I thought his offer was an opportunity too good to miss. It would be heaven, I thought, to live so close to civilisation. With the bitumen road only forty miles away from the station it would be easy for me to drive into Katherine and back in a day.

I told George of Ron Ryan's offer, but didn't dwell on it. I knew George liked the Mt. Sanford country and had no thought of leaving, but I'd had more than enough of isolation, and it was time to think of the children and myself for a change. I couldn't rid myself of the feeling that while I was in this backwater, life was rushing by and leaving me behind. I also wanted my children to have as good an education as I'd had, but not at the expense of a normal family life.

When the mustering was nearly finished, George took the Landrover and all the men down to VRD for a few days' break. Once again I was left behind, which was very hurtful, and once again I shed a few tears. I hadn't seen another white woman for about six months, nor had I seen the children. I was heartily sick of the sight of men and hearing men's talk. How I would have loved a nice cup of tea and a chat with a woman that could not be overheard for miles around. As for the children, well what could I say?

George returned a few days later and told me that Mr Quirk was furious with me, but he didn't know what about. He thought it was a great joke, but I was mystified! What could I possibly have said or done to upset him? Within a week the stock camp had moved out, and a few days later I received a radio message that Quirk was on his way to see me. He arrived in time for afternoon tea and after this was over he began to question me about Ron Ryan's visit – what had actually been said, was I dissatisfied with the rations, and so on. I explained that although some items had been cut out, these were more in the way of luxuries than necessities, but the potatoes and onions we really missed. He then asked if dehydrated ones would be acceptable and I agreed that they'd probably be much better.

Next I was asked about the tonnage that had come into the VRD store when I was the storekeeper there. I answered truthfully that I had no idea because at that time I'd only been interested in the loading which came into the store, checking this with the cart notes and the cart notes against the invoices. My sister was the bookkeeper in the office at that time and she'd attended to everything else. I presumed that the total cartage now would be less because in that year several windmills, several new buildings and roofing iron had arrived, as well as new furniture for the big house.

He nodded his head as if satisfied, then began to query me on just what I'd told Ron Ryan about the Aboriginals' meals. I explained that other than the fruit and vegetables we grew in the garden there was now very little extra, and that the Aboriginals no longer received much more than the prescribed Government rations. I said that I'd appreciate it if once again garden seeds could be supplied each year as they were of great benefit to everyone, and he agreed to this. He then stared hard at me for a moment, gave a satisfied hurrumphing cough, and left.

Some weeks later there were wild stories going around – Quirk was supposed to have sacked old Jack McDonald from Pigeon Hole and the Martin Brothers were said to have lost the VRD contract. The Martins had carried all the stores from the Alice Springs railhead to VRD ever since I'd been on the station. This had been their mainstay and it wasn't very long before they went out of business. Eventually I found out that Ron Ryan and Stan Martin had both been at Pigeon Hole at the same time before Ron came to Mt. Sanford. Evidently Stan was bewailing the decline in the amount of business and Big Mack was bewailing the loss of the rations. Ron could see a good chance to have a go at Jack Quirk about the decline in maintenance of the Aboriginals, and they decided to use me as a scapegoat.

A few months later the mustering finished. When the Kings Cross Ringers got their wage cheques I don't think either of them had ever had so much money before, and they decided to return home to Sydney. George told me that we were also going down South for a holiday and I decided it was time to put my foot down. I replied that I'd had enough of Mt. Sanford and that the children and I wouldn't be coming back again. Of course, this was a bluff. I don't know what I could have done or where I would have gone if he'd ignored me. George never said a word. He just walked off, but I packed up everything we owned in the hope that he'd take the Beswick job. Once again my fate was up in the air.

Within a few days I'd loaded the Landrover with all our worldly goods and the Kings Cross Ringers got up on top on the swags. The children and I said a tearful farewell to the girls as they hugged and kissed us because we knew we might never see any of them again. We set off for VRD to pick up our cheques and then continued on to Katherine. There George saw Ron Ryan and accepted the position at Beswick station. 'Whoopie!' I thought, but I didn't say a word. After all, I'd got what I wanted. I wouldn't have far to go to civilisation and I could arrange to have correspondence lessons sent up from Adelaide for the children.

At Katherine we unloaded a lot of our gear so that it could be sent out to Beswick. Then we drove up to Darwin where we traded in the Landrover for a new EJ Holden. George had offered to drive the two boys to Sydney so we had a full carload as we set off. George, Erica and I were in the front, and the two boys and the other children in the back. The boot and luggage rack was piled high with our swags and camping gear. We were off on the first leg of a 10,000 mile round trip through Queensland,

New South Wales and Victoria, and across to Adelaide to spend Christmas with my family. On the way down everyone was given strict instructions to speak only plain English to Erica. She was fluent in the Mt. Sanford Aboriginal dialect and in 'pidgin', but not in English. I knew my mother would be horrified at this so Erica was given a crash course, and by the time we reached Adelaide she spoke English very well. Goodness knows what mum would have said if she hadn't!

When we arrived in Adelaide we found Natalie was there too, and our sister Gwenda had decided to hold a Christmas Dinner for all the family, the first time we'd all been together since the beginning of the Second World War. This was the Christmas of 1958. After a couple of weeks we said our goodbyes and started on our return journey via Alice Springs. I wondered what our new home at Beswick would be like and how I'd get on with the Aboriginals there. My official position was to be Cook/Matron. I'd have to supervise the Aboriginal cook in the large kitchen/ dining room, and see to the wellbeing of everyone. Little did I know just what I'd let myself in for, but that's another story!

Recipes of a Bush Cook

Mock Bush Turkey

A rib roll roast of beef.
1 tin of Kraft cheese (grated).
1 good handful of seeded raisins.

Sprinkle cheese and raisins over the meat. Roll up into a round roast. Secure with string or meat skewers. Roast in the usual way.

Over the years I've fooled quite a few old Territorians with this recipe. They were convinced that I was serving them wild bush turkey. They wouldn't believe me when I told them it was ordinary beef. Turkeys are protected, but it was quite common for people to vow that the bird had flown into the path of their vehicle and been injured, so they had had to put it out of its misery, and this was obviously what they thought that I had done.

As beef was the only meat one saw, three times a day, seven days a week, any variation was really appreciated. This was why my Bush Turkey was so popular. While at Mt. Sanford we did occasionally kill a goat, but with so many people it did not go far. Here is another variation.

Baked steak

2lbs of stewing steak
1 teaspoon of sugar
1 teaspoon of Holbrook's sauce
1 tablespoon of vinegar
A grating of nutmeg
1 teaspoon of salt
1 teaspoonful of pepper
1 tablespoon of Tomato sauce
3 cups of water
1 tablespoonful of plain flour.

Mix all ingredients together except the flour. Pour over the steak. Let stand for one hour. Bake in a casserole over 2 hours (or it can be cooked in a saucepan). When cooked, thicken the gravy with the flour.

Beef Shape

2lbs of shin of beef, with the bone
1 large onion
4 cloves
1 teaspoonful of thyme
pepper and salt.

Wipe the meat and cut off the bone. Put bone and meat in a large saucepan with flavourings. Add enough cold water to just cover. Bring to the boil and simmer for 3-4 hours, until the meat is quite tender. Allow to cool. Remove fat from the top, cut meat into small pieces and season with salt and pepper. Add a teaspoonful of chopped parsley if you have some and place all into a greased mould. Strain the liquid and add to mould. When cold and set, turn out and serve with salads.

Eggless Fruit Cake (when the chooks are on strike.)

8 oz of clean dripping
6 oz sugar
2 heaped tablespoons of custard powder
6 oz of plain flour
Cream of tartar
Baking soda (or powder)
Half a pannikin of milk
1 teaspoon of vanilla essence
a handful each of raisins, sultanas, currants and a little citrus peel if available

Beat the butter and sugar to a cream. Sift the custard powder, flour and baking powder together, three times for extra lightness.

Add two tablespoonful of the flour mixture to the fruit and add to the creamed mixture. Then add flour and milk alternatively until the mixture is a good dropping consistency.

Pour into a prepared baking dish and cook in a moderate oven until the top is a golden brown and a testing skewer comes out clean.

I sometimes varied this recipe by omitting the fruit and adding vanilla or lemon flavouring.

Sago Plum Pudding (the Ringer's Delight.)

I had to make three at a time to go around.

1 cup of fresh bread crumbs
2 scant tablespoons of Sago,
Half a cup of sugar
1 teaspoonful of lemon essence
1 cup of milk
1 cup of sultanas
A quarter of a teaspoonful of nutmeg
1 teaspoonful of cold water
Half a level teaspoon of bicarbonate of soda
1 small egg (or dessertspoonful of custard powder.)
2 tablespoons of butter or dripping (3 if custard powder is used.)

Heat the milk and pour over the breadcrumbs, sago, and butter. Allow it to stand for half an hour. Add the sugar, fruit, nutmeg and essence. Dissolve the soda in the water and add to mixture. Beat the egg and stir in lightly, but thoroughly. Pour into a greased basin, place greased paper on top and secure tightly with string. Steam for 2½ hours. Serve with cream or custard.

Mother's Apple Cake (This is older than I am.)

2 cups of plain flour
4 teaspoons full of mixed spice
4 cooking apples (I used dried apples)
1 heaped teaspoonful of baking powder (or use self raising flour)
1/4 lb of butter or clean dripping
1 cup of sugar
2 eggs
1 tablespoonful of sugar

Cook apples and sugar and cool. Mix flour, sugar and spice together. Rub in the butter. Beat the eggs and mix in. Grease a sandwich tin and line with the pastry (it is fairly moist, so take care). Put in the cooled apples and top with the remaining mixture.

Cook for about half an hour in a moderate oven. Ice while warm, sprinkle the top with cinnamon, serve warm or cold with custard or cream.

Confectioner's Cream

Dissolve 2oz sugar in a cup of hot water. Whisk together in a bowl, 1oz of flour, 1oz sugar, 2 tablespoonful cold water. Add the hot syrup to this mixture. Stirring, return to the stove and cook until semi-transparent. When the gel is cold, cream 4oz butter (unsalted if available) until quite light. Gradually add the gel. Flavour with vanilla essence.

Roly-Poly Pudding (I made three times this amount.)

4 oz of plain flour
1 tablespoon sugar
Water
4 oz of suet
A pinch of salt

Rub the flour, suet and sugar together, add enough water to make a dry dough. Roll out into a sausage shape. Roll up in a floured cloth and tie ends tightly. Place into a pot of boiling water for 2 to 2½ hours. Add more boiling water during cooking as necessary. Roll out onto serving plate. Serve with golden syrup and cream or custard.

Easy Custard

Mix 4 heaped tablespoons of Sunshine Powdered Milk with 1 tablespoon of sugar and 1 tablespoon of custard powder with a little water, just enough to be able to blend it all smoothly together. While beating, add boiling water until custard is the desired consistency. No more milk boiling over on the stove! Another tip, the more milk you use the creamier the custard.

Puftaloons

Mix together self raising flour with enough water to form a batter which will drop easily off the end of a spoon. Drop a tablespoonful of it into deep fat until golden brown. Turn halfway if the fat is not deep enough for them to turn on their own. Cook in batches. Split in halves and fill with golden syrup and cream. An egg may be added to this batter, but I was often without eggs.

This mixture is also very nice as dumplings, cooked on top of a casserole or stew for the last 10 minutes.

Blue Boiler Peas (When no fresh vegetables are available)

Place a quantity of dried peas in an empty flour or sugar bag. Soak in water for a half an hour. Hang up in a cool place. Re-wet the bag every day until peas begin to sprout. They are then ready to use as ordinary green peas. The same can be done with Haricot beans.

Another trick I learnt was to utilise the oven or the wood stove by cooking the vegetables in a baking dish of water while the fire was low during the afternoon. All root vegetables, potatoes and onions cook well this way. I put them all in together in one big dish.

Quick Sponge

4 eggs 8 oz sugar
6 oz self raising flour (or 4 oz self raising and 2 oz corn flour),
2 tablespoons boiling water.

Beat sugar and eggs together for 10 minutes. Add boiling water, then add flour, sifted three times, stir very lightly. Bake in sponge tins in moderate oven for 15–20 minutes. Fill with jam and cream. I often used wild passion fruit for this, instead of jam.

I grease and line my tins with paper, raising the sides well above the tins. Grease the paper, then lightly flour. I find the cakes always rise well over the top of the tins. Another tip: If the weather is cool, place the mixing bowl of eggs and sugar into a large saucepan, which has some boiling water in it. The mixture will cream better, But don't let the bowl touch the water. Remove bowl from saucepan before adding the flour.

Because we had a vegetable garden I usually had a good crop of tomatoes. With these I occasionally made the following recipe.

Mock Chicken

2 large ripe tomatoes — 1 small onion
1 slice of butter — 1 teaspoon of thyme
2 slices of bread (crumbed) — Pepper and salt to taste
1/4 lb of cheese (I used Kraft tinned cheddar as it was all I had available)

Peel tomatoes and cut finely. Slice onion finely. Grate the cheese. Mix all the ingredients together and boil for 6 minutes, stirring all the time while cooking.

Put into jars and cover with melted butter. Use on sandwiches and savoury biscuits.

Burdekin Duck

6 tablespoons of self raising flour — 1 egg
Sufficient water to make a batter.
Slices of cold meat (salt beef was always used in the bush)

Mix all ingredients together, coat the slices with the batter and fry on each side until golden brown.

This same batter mixture I used to make fruit slices. As I only had dried fruit I'd soak the fruit in water over night and dust them with sugar when cooked. Serve with custard.

Dumplings can also be made from this mixture. Just use a little less water so that it's more the consistency of scone dough. Drop spoonsfull into a stew and cook for the last ten minutes.

Apricot Brandy

I always kept a small bottle of brandy for emergencies and decided to try the following recipe. Take 8 ounces of apricots (or any dried fruit). Place in a saucepan with 4½ pints of water. Simmer slowly until the fruit is very soft. Allow to cool, pour strained liquid into a bottle. Add a cup of brandy to each bottle and cork tightly. Leave to mature for at least three months. Yummy! The fruit may be eaten after some sugar has been added to sweeten it.

Index

C

D

E

F

G

H

I

J

K

L

T

V

W

Y

Z